Improving Work Groups

A Practical Manual for Team Building

by
Dave Francis
Don Young

University Associates
8517 Production Avenue
P.O. Box 26240
San Diego, California
92126

Contents

Foreword

It is a particular pleasure to write a few words of introduction to this book by Dave Francis and Don Young because I have worked extensively with both of them and we share many beliefs and values about the development of effective teamwork. From personal experience I know that both Dave and Don have great skills in helping organizations become more effective, and this book captures many of the techniques they regularly use in their work. In addition, the book is a companion volume to *Unblocking Your Organization* (University Associates, 1979), which is a revised edition of *People at Work: A Practical Guide to Organization Change,* written by Dave and myself.

But it is not for these reasons that I commend the approach to you. It is because I share the authors' view that guidance on organization team building is much needed and long overdue and I believe that this book comprehensively covers the field. Increasingly, successful organizations are those with people who can work effectively together. Readers who wish to help that process will find in this book a wealth of practical explanation and ideas.

I hope that you find *Improving Work Groups: A Practical Manual for Team Building* as stimulating, enjoyable, and useful as I have.

Mike Woodcock
Organization Consultant
and Managing Director,
University Associates of Europe

Preface

The effectiveness of an organization is greatly influenced by the quality of cooperation among its groups and among its individual members. For this reason, many large businesses have been spending large budgets on team training. Their efforts have reaped a harvest of know-how about team building, which can be applied in all forms of organizations.

We have inherited that knowledge and skill. The team-building techniques described in this book already have been used by many diverse organizations, including commercial companies, sports teams, religious communities, and community service organizations. We encourage you to adapt these techniques creatively and extend them to new areas.

This book has wide implications for organizations. A friend of ours, talking about a multinational corporation, said, "The great thing about this company is that it has a culture that helps the average manager perform at an above-average level." There is depth in this remark. He identified a mysterious "something" in the work teams of an organization that brings strength to individuals. We hope that you will join us in searching for this "something."

Like marriage, team building promises much but can go wrong—it makes demands on each participant. All who participate in team building must be prepared to open their minds to new ideas and experiences. Only a willingness to work through old issues and build new relationships can make the team approach work.

This exploration of the team's primary work and relationships must be handled with much care. If you choose to do this, then this book can make a positive, strong, and creative intervention into the life of your team.

Since this book is written for those who are "on the line," we have tried to present ideas in a direct and easily read manner. You will find no statements such as "preliminary indications suggest that a tentative hypothesis, subject to further research clarification, is . . . " However, we have included the practical outcomes of current research and, as far as we know, our suggestions are in line with current behaviorial science research.

Practical books on team building are long overdue. We hope this work helps to meet that need and that it encourages you to innovate and to add the essential flesh to these bones.

ACKNOWLEDGMENTS

Reflecting on those who contributed to this book, we find that we owe more to the world of action rather than to research. We are particularly grateful to practitioners Peter Samuel, John Halpin, Bob Rogers, Pat Maule, Alan Savage, Mick Crews, and Bert Medlam, and also to Bill Pfeiffer, John Jones, Roger Harrison, and Barry Goodfield, whose ideas have meant a great deal. An initial inspiration of great value came from the training ideas developed by E. R. Danzig and E. C. Nevis. We also thank our editor, Phyllis Russell, who sharpened our text, structured our thinking and struggled with our British spelling.

This book is similar in structure to *Unblocking Your Organization,* and we recognize the strong contribution that Mike Woodcock made to our way of writing. Another colleague, Celia Palfreyman, contributed many ideas and suggestions that helped us considerably.

We also owe a lot to Maureen Young, Pauline Wyatt-Ingram, Lois Kelly, and Shirley Jackson for typing, editing, and generally keeping us in line. However, the responsibility for blemishes, errors, and biases rests with the authors.

Lastly, we invite you, our readers, to tell us how you use this book in practice. You may write to us in care of our publisher.

Richmond, Surrey   *Dave Francis*
England   *Don Young*

1

The Team-Building Process

How To Use This Book

This is a practical handbook for those who wish to develop the creative and productive potential of the human group. It is a book about *teams*. Teams can be intentionally built and the skills that enable this process to happen also can be developed. We have designed this step-by-step manual to help the reader acquire the skills needed for developing effective teams.

THE TEAM MANAGER

This book is directed toward the person who is practically concerned with developing team effectiveness. This may be a team member or a team-development agent, but it usually is the person "in charge." This *team manager* has a vital part to play in developing a team-management approach. We see this as a distinctive management style; it requires a commitment to *developing* the resources of the group rather than to *controlling* it like a master puppeteer.

Reflect for a moment on your own management style. Do you see your role mainly as a builder or a controller? How consistent are you in that role? These questions will help you to evaluate whether the team approach is relevant to your personal style.

Team management is not an easy option or an abdication of responsibility. It contrasts with the political gamester approach to management, in which the skills required are those of manipulation and subtle control. The team manager builds openness and risks development, while trying to utilize energy and harness initiative.

OUR BIASES AND YOUR ATTITUDES

This is a partisan book. It reflects our belief that a team approach is a relevant, timely, humane, and effective way to get things done. The team-management style is a positive way to manage tomorrow's organizations and channel the energies of those who work within them.

We invite you to monitor your own reactions as you read; at times you may find yourself nodding in agreement or frowning with displeasure. This can be useful information because it reveals your attitudes and can clarify your own position and beliefs.

STRUCTURE OF THE BOOK

The somewhat unusual structure of this book blends explanation and ideas with the practical tools you need to build your team. The following outline should clarify the structure.

FUNCTION	CONTENTS
Part 1	
Understanding team building	What is a team?
	Why build teams?
	How to build teams?
	Who builds teams?
Part 2	
Surveying your own team	Team-review questionnaire
Part 3	
Describing characteristics of effective teams	Twelve key areas to develop
Part 4	
Improving your own team	Forty-six projects to use in practice with your team

Part 1. We begin the book by explaining team building in some depth, with the purpose of providing a foundation of ideas to get you started. Part 1 offers guidelines, identifies opportunities, and makes some cautionary statements. Towards the end of Part 1 we move from general principles into practical application and invite you to survey your own team.

Part 2. The Team-Review Questionnaire is used to identify the strengths and weaknesses of your team, and it provides more objective information than can be gathered in other ways.

Part 3. Having assessed your own team, you can move on to Part 3, which explores the many learnable skills that help team members effectively work through problems.

Part 4. The projects in Part 4 are specific suggestions for actions to help you progress with team building. This is your tool bag. Each project is a guided experiment—a structured experience—for your team to undertake. The activities are described in detail and step-by-step procedures should enable many of them to be undertaken without outside help. Through experience, your team should gather the insight and skills needed to work through the blocks inhibiting your team.

THE TEAM-BUILDING PROCESS

Few teams develop to their full effectiveness without a good deal of nurturing and conscious development. The team-building processes outlined in this book are aimed at bringing an element of open, systematic planning and review to the task of developing teams. However, experience tells us that team development cannot be fully planned and predicted through a rigidly programed approach. Instead, there will be spurts of progress and apparent relapses; new insights will develop along the way, and carefully formulated programs will be changed.

It is wise, therefore, as you plan the development of your team, not to let the plan become a straight jacket. The team's experiences can be used to guide behavior and to predict future needs. Value your feelings equally with your intellectual analyses.

This book can help you to start and progress with team building, but a special ingredient is needed that only you can add—your own energy, insights, and skills.

Team Building: What, Why, How

The team approach is a distinctive style of working aimed at harnessing the collective talent and energy of people. The concept is particularly relevant to our time. Many organizations are confronted externally with complex, turbulent environments and internally with lassitude and dissent. Many managers in such organizations are seeking a positive management philosophy that achieves useful results and, at the same time, respects the needs of employees. The team approach described in this book is designed for their use. It is a flexible tool that emphasizes exploration and self-development through experience.

Although managers speak of teams and teamwork, they often are vague about the precise meaning of the words. It is important to become clear about the benefits and distinctive characteristics of a team approach.

WHAT IS A TEAM?

While researching for this book, we asked several hundred managers to define an effective team from their own experience. This survey revealed two characteristics as almost universally recognized by managers.

- Effective teams produce outstanding results and succeed in achieving despite difficulties.
- Members feel responsible for the output of their team and act to clear difficulties standing in their way.

The managers recognized that an effective team skillfully combines appropriate individual talents with a positive team spirit to achieve results. A team, therefore, is more than a collection of individuals. It is, in part, an emotional entity, rooted in the feelings as well as the thoughts of its members; they actively care about their team's well-being.

Examined more scientifically, a team is a human group, but not all groups qualify as teams. There are times when a work group is used by individuals to achieve personal ends or to protect themselves. At other times, committees can stifle creativity and blunt decision making. Many managers rightly complain that meetings are "a unique blend of boredom, time wasting, and muddle-headed decisions."

Occasionally, we meet an exceptional group that combines high morale, effective task performance, and clear relevance to the organization and we award it the accolade of a "team."

Characteristics of an Effective Team

It is useful to look at some specific characteristics of a team in more detail. They are: output, objectives, energy, structure, and atmosphere.

Output. The test of a team is its capacity to deliver the goods. A team is capable of achieving results that the individuals who comprise it cannot do in isolation. Their diverse talents combine in the team to create an end product beyond their individual capability.

Objectives. A team needs a purpose that is understood, shared, and felt to be worthwhile by its members. This purpose can be described as the team's "mission." In addition, there will be specific objectives that the team and each individual member have a commitment to achieve. Mature teams draw strength and direction from a shared understanding of a common purpose and from identification of how each member's objectives contribute towards the achievement of that purpose.

Energy. Team members take strength from one another. Collectively, they feel more potent and find that team activities renew their vitality and enjoyment. The word synergy was coined to describe this special group energy. Synergy has been explained with the mathematically improbable, but psychologically accurate, equation: $2 + 2 = 5$. A team does have a character and capacity beyond the sum of its individual members. It has a capacity for synergy, a group energy that can be deliberately developed and utilized.

Structure. A mature team has dealt with thorny questions concerned with control, leadership, procedures, organization, and roles. The team's structure is finely attuned to tasks being undertaken, and individual talents and contributions are utilized without confusion. Team members with a drive for leadership have learned to understand each other and to cope with any feelings of hostility, competitiveness, or aggression. The team has managed to become flexible, responsive, orderly, and directed.

Atmosphere. A team develops a distinctive spirit. This team spirit allows for openness between the members, and for their support and simple enjoyment of one another. Team members identify themselves with the team and its success or failure affects their feelings. They will extend themselves to serve the interests of the team. Such a team develops an atmosphere within which confidences can be shared, personal difficulties worked through, and risks undertaken.

Defining a Team

Based on our analysis, we can define a team as: *An energetic group of people who are committed to achieving common objectives, who work well together and enjoy doing so, and who produce high quality results.* According to the definition, a team consists of individuals who relate directly together to get things done. This suggests a practical limitation on size, because rarely in practice can more than nine people function as a single team.

However, some of the characteristics of teamwork can be cultivated in much larger groups. Departments and even whole enterprises can adopt a team concept as a management style. Once trained and committed, people see that fluid teams can be formed as the need arises, and they try to extend the team approach outside the closed boundary of their own teams. A whole organization can in certain respects be similar to a gigantic team.

WHAT IS TEAM BUILDING?

Learning is generally thought of as an individual pursuit, but this is only partly true. Teams also learn and their skills are the property of the group as a whole. Watch a first-class football game or an astronaut crew, and you will see highly advanced team ability.

The process of deliberately creating a team is called *team building.* The expression is useful because it suggests something substantial that has to be constructed and that will go through several stages and take time to complete.

We have identified an elusive but crucial level of collective learning that is the core of team building. Teams have to find answers to seven questions:

1. What are we here to do?
2. How shall we organize ourselves?
3. Who is in charge?
4. Who cares about our success?
5. How do we work through problems?
6. How do we fit in with other groups?
7. What benefits do team members need from the team?

These questions are not answered in a step-by-step process. In practice, issues are worked through as they become significant blockages to progress. If a blockage is worked through successfully, then the team becomes stronger. If the blockage is not cleared, then the team regresses.

Team building involves the deliberate working through of all blockages to progress until a working group becomes an effective team. The idea of clearing blockages (more extensively developed in later chapters) is the most important tool in our approach to team building. Another important idea is expressed by the term *working through,* because time and focused effort is required to resolve blockages.

Stages of Team Development

Teams have a process of growth that can be understood and described, although the stages of team development do not follow a predictable step-by-step evolutionary sequence like a caterpillar transforming into a butterfly. There is more variety in human affairs. Nonetheless, a clear pattern can be detected as a loose assembly of individuals goes through the developmental obstacle course and emerges as a team.

STAGE 1. TESTING

People react very differently to the challenge of meeting new colleagues. Some are fearful and have sweating palms and dry lips. Others are eager, looking forward to opportunities for excitement, achievement, and challenge. There also may be someone who is evasive, disgruntled, attention seeking, or morose. The possible combinations are endless.

It is with this foundation that the team begins to form. People initially seek to find their place in a group in relation to others. Their psychological antennae are fully tuned, often to the subtle, nonverbal messages that individuals constantly monitor. Each person is trying to answer a personal question: "How do I belong to this group?" Each person proceeds with personal, conventional ways of getting involved with others. For example, some people hang back as observers until they feel comfortable, while others dash in with a frenzy of good humor and amiable conversation.

As the team begins to form, there is a gradual growth of personal exchange and contact. People seek to find out about one another, wanting to uncover attitudes, values, style, and the other person's readiness to be contacted. This testing process continues until each person makes a decision concerning the character of his or her involvement.

At this stage, the team may appear to be acting effectively, progressing with its tasks and forming what seems to be a friendly comradeship between members. However, this condition often is only skin-deep, because the initial effectiveness comes from attitudes and training established prior to the team being formed. A team should enable each person to get to know the other members in a less superficial way. As a result, the initial comfort of the members may disappear as more real issues bubble to the surface.

STAGE 2. INFIGHTING

As the team develops, it becomes necessary to sort out personal relationships of power and influence. Alliances are formed and certain people emerge as particularly significant.

The team manager has particular authority because the organization has recognized his significant contribution. Yet this special position must be earned. Team members watch and evaluate the manager's behavior, and they may accept his leadership or find cunning ways to evade it.

At this stage, the team has to decide how it is going to operate. All too often this is done by subterranean rumbling but with little explicit planning. In essence, all the issues are concerned with control, and three questions are dominant:

1. Who controls the team?
2. How is control exercised?
3. What happens to "delinquents"?

The team has to find an answer to each of these questions if it is to proceed. There are no straightforward remedies. Difficulties facing the team must be confronted or evaded. Some teams fail to find ways of satisfactorily working through control difficulties. This acts as a permanent block and although the team may appear to make progress, underneath there is a fundamental weakness.

STAGE 3. GETTING ORGANIZED

Following the successful resolution (for the time being at least!) of the issues surrounding control, the team begins to tackle its work with a new energy. People want to work together and have committed themselves to trying to make the team work. This is an important stage because the team needs the support and interest of all members. Without this, individual preoccupations dominate, and the team itself fails to grow stronger.

The work of the team becomes identified with precision, and contribution is discussed and measured. Typically, the quality of listening improves and people begin to respect each other's contribution. Team members become more concerned with economy of effort and task effectiveness. Shorthand ways of talking develop, and considerable time is spent reviewing performance and identifying new options.

At this stage the team has to grow in its capacity to handle problems creatively, flexibly, and effectively. Without this evolution of working methods, the team will continue using barely effective modes of operating, satisfying itself with adequate effectiveness rather than striving towards being excellent.

Getting organized inevitably takes time. Depth of understanding between people needs to be developed and approaches to problem solving need to be shared, so that consistent disciplines are established and objectives are rigorously clarified.

STAGE 4. MATURE CLOSENESS

The members of a fully established team develop rapport and closeness. Sometimes this is so strong that indelible bonds of comradeship are forged. Team members are prepared to extend themselves for their colleagues and real enjoyment of each other is typical.

Informality is often a keynote of a team at this stage, but it is based on positive regard for each of the other team members. There is a strong feeling that others would be willing to help if needed. Roles of team members have been identified and each person's contribution is distinctive.

Observers of the team are aware of the team's close bonds, but team members also build close and open links with those outside the team. Aware that it is difficult to avoid negative rumors and images from developing, team members take steps to reduce the risk that the closeness of the team can feed arrogance and insular attitudes.

Definite steps have been taken to clarify the team's organization role and contribution. A mature team does not allow its function to become redundant or obscure; it will influence others to provide the recognition and support needed. In the same way that a disadvantaged group learns to make its voice heard, so also does a team gain sufficient strength to ensure that it assertively puts its case across.

WHY DO IT?

The Needs of Today's Organizations

Many managers yearn for the old days in which markets were relatively stable, the dispatch of a gunboat could quell problems overseas, and staff would jump obediently to a crisp order. In those times, the overriding need was to create organizations that were stable, hierarchical, and as efficient as clockwork machines.

Now organizations are experiencing environmental forces that are rapidly changing and increasingly unpredictable—forces such as international and domestic politics, social attitudes, market and consumer preferences, and financial trends. It has been said that "turbulence is now the stable state." This has profound implications for styles of management. In addition to ensuring *control,* which has been required since the pyramids were built, there is the need to manage creatively the processes of *adaptation* and *innovation.*

Management has rediscovered a half-forgotten idea; the individual is crucial in directing or withholding decisions, services, skills or energy. Belief in the sacrosanct superiority of institutional heads is waning. Since social forces weaken authority, the individual now has to be involved by a management that strives to combine wide corporate objectives with individual aspirations. The importance of the individual in organizations is expanded by political changes, legal requirements, and, above all, by a rising consciousness that each person has potential and choice.

People are now better educated, more libertarian, and less romantic about the ideal of progress. They are less willing to work diligently and conform to rules. Traditionally, managers have depended on this willingness to manage situations. This is made clear by examining the role of one level of management.

A look at the role of the supervisor shows clearly how the attitudinal changes toward work, education, technology, and life-style have resulted in more tension and stress. A supervisor is expected to produce consistently better results while, almost without exception, each new social and technological trend has made life more difficult.

The cost of industrial action is often so high that senior managers are driven towards a policy of appeasement over apparently minor issues such as discipline. Of course, this is logical from their point of view, but the consequences for the supervisor, the person who is supposed to uphold discipline, often are invidious.

Here is a fairly typical example. A supervisor has decided to discipline an employee who persistently takes overlong break periods. On a day when the employee returns ten minutes later than the time allowed, the supervisor fines him a quarter of an hour's pay. The employee complains to his representative, who takes up his case with the excuse that the lateness was justified because of a delay in the cafeteria and that, argues the representative, is the responsibility of management.

The supervisor, knowing that this employee's lateness is part of a regular pattern, does not relent, and the company grievance procedure takes the issue to a higher level. Here the more senior managers, fearing the consequences of industrial action, ask themselves, "Is it worth stopping a twenty-million-dollar plant for fifteen minutes' pay?" Their answer is negative, the supervisor's decision is reversed, and the employee enjoys his victory. The representative has become a little more powerful and credible to the employees, the supervisor a little less powerful and credible. It does not take many incidents like this before the supervisor feels unsupported and confused.

Supervisors are questioning what their role should be; they are noting that their role has to be played in a different way. No longer are military leaders the oracles of business management style. Instead, management is being influenced by people who preach trust, openness, understanding, and participation. However, these new styles of management demand greater personal strengths and skills than the old, and any manager who adopts them without sufficient understanding and concern for people is likely to fail.

Supervisors who use the team-building approach have a clearer, more potent, and practical management philosophy to guide them. As a consequence, they develop skills to increase the openness, commitment, and problem-solving ability of their work team. Issues of discipline are clarified and are less likely to degenerate into an "us" against "them" conflict. As self-regulation increases in the team, fewer problems emerge. The work done to build a positive team spirit bears fruit in the form of good will.

Using the team-building approach reveals the supervisor, to himself and to others, as making a significant contribution to the organization and as having a creative role that catches the imagination. Such a supervisor is re-evaluated by senior managers, who begin taking more care with their communication and with providing resources.

The development of a management team that includes the work-team supervisors as members provides each supervisor with dual roles as a team manager and a team member. The supervisors' participation in both teams offers the most practical framework for resolving issues as they occur and for minimizing destructive effects of problems. Their participation on the management team also reduces the distressed impotence expressed by many supervisors and channels their energy more positively. The dual roles of the supervisors are illustrated in the diagram shown in Figure 1.

Motives for Team Building

It is important to understand the motives that people have for initiating a team-building venture. The following are some examples of managers whose intention is positive and who are likely to succeed:

- A newly appointed manager who wants to achieve rapid acceptance in an established group;

- A pragmatic manager who wants to use team building to further an open, problem-solving approach to management;

- A manager facing new challenges and demands who needs the creativity and commitment of those involved to handle the job;

- A manager facing problems of relationship, commitment, or lack of clarity who needs to break out of the doldrums.

Team building sometimes is undertaken for more negative reasons and the results frequently are disappointing, for example:

- Team building may be initiated by a remote instruction from the corporate head office without the support of those directly involved;

- A manager may undertake team building with the intention of increasing his capacity to manipulate and control. This is contrary to the values that are the foundation of the team-building approach.

The process of linking people to achieve results that matter to them is central to the team approach. The main requirement that must be met before a team-building program begins is that all members of the team have freely agreed to undertake the development steps required. This should be a decision taken without pressure but with information. In practice, we have seen no ill effects when groups have applied our techniques on the basis of voluntary participation. Team-building techniques are powerful and can be abused; they should not be imposed from without.

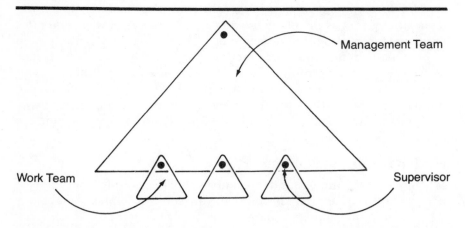

Figure 1. Dual roles of supervisors

Benefits of Team Building

The team, potentially the most flexible and competent tool known to mankind, can support a positive management strategy in the following ways:

- *Management of Complexity.* The breadth of resources available to the team enables complex situations to be creatively managed.
- *Rapid Response.* Well-developed teams are capable of responding quickly and energetically.
- *High Motivation.* The team feeds the individual's need to have personal significance, and team processes encourage activity and achievement.
- *High Quality Decisions.* Mature teams are capable of making better quality decisions than all but the most brilliant individual. Hence, the use of a team approach improves the overall quality of decisions. Perhaps more importantly, the level of commitment to team decisions is much higher.
- *Collective Strength.* Individuals often feel that it is hard to influence organizations and make any impact outside their immediate area. The team changes this as team members extend their viewpoint to see that they, together, can achieve much.

Who Can Benefit From Team Building?

Team building is time consuming and can be expensive. It is important to identify how the approach can be used to give useful benefits.

INDIVIDUALS

However effective, management education and training is not the real world. Managers often have great difficulties in transferring their newly learned management skills back into the work situation because group standards reinforce old ways of working. When individuals are thwarted in their efforts to accomplish improvement, then positive energy turns sour. An organization can end up with a frustrated, disgruntled manager who has acquired better tools for assessing the validity of his own dissatisfaction.

These disadvantages in individual-centered approaches are much less when the work group is the unit of intervention and learning. Then learning can occur in daily practice and can bring about real change in areas that matter. When a team devises new ways of tackling real problems, the members have a useful learning experience and develop new skills that can be drawn on again and again.

Individuals are able to develop their personal skills through team-building experiences. They become more competent in working with others to effectively solve problems. Team building broadens the concept of leadership and gives practice in developing a supportive open climate.

We know of one competent technical manager who was assigned to head a major subsidiary a few weeks after he went through a team-skills training session. After six months he said, "If I had not experienced the training, I would have handled the assignment entirely differently. I set up project and review teams all over the place, whereas previously I would have dealt with individuals separately. Now I have their commitment."

TOP-MANAGEMENT TEAMS

Teams of top managers often are the major link between the organization and its external environment. They must assess what is going on outside, predict the effects on the organization as a whole, and make hard decisions about the organization's responses. These functions require a far-sighted and imaginative appraisal of complex issues that are beyond the scope of most individuals working alone.

Top managers then must join effectively with others in the organization to ensure that broad goals are translated into energetic and focused activity. If comments are heard from inside the organization, such as "I don't know what that bunch up there think they are doing" and "Anybody with half an eye could have seen this problem coming," then top-management teams are not working well.

Most top managers are survivors; they watch out for themselves and are careful who they trust. In this respect, organizations change little over the centuries. The politics of top-management groups can be extremely destructive to the well-being of the organization. It is naive to believe that politics can be eradicated; however, it is practical to work towards a more open confrontation of the issues involved.

These two topics, managing complexity and organizational politics, are particularly important in top-management team building.

MANAGEMENT TEAMS

Management teams—usually a manager and those who report to him—most commonly undertake team building. Such teams are relatively stable and handle a wide variety of assignments, e.g. running a factory, department, or service facility. The quality of relationships between team members can affect large numbers of people who look to the team to provide clear and energetic direction.

PROJECT TEAMS

Many organizations are using project teams to solve problems quickly or to develop new processes or products. Such teams may get together for only a few weeks or for years at a time. Project teams can be extended across the organization so that many individuals report to more than one boss. Collectively the teams are responsible for achieving some significant objective, and it is here that the team-management approach offers major benefits.

It is necessary for project managers to collect together a mix of skills that can technically handle the project, and they also must create enough drive and enthusiasm to see the project through. Difficult decisions often have to be made on uncertain data, and a well-developed team can use the varied talents of team members in making effective decisions. This form of decision making, so well displayed by members of the Apollo space program, has significant advantages when the team is well-developed and mature. However, in the hands of immature teams this method becomes a recipe for incompetence and confusion. Team-building techniques are relevant, probably essential, to enable project teams to work effectively.

An electronics organization obtained an order for a fifty-million-dollar radar installation that had to be completed over a tight two-year time scale. All the senior project managers met off-site for a one-week team-building session during which they identified more than one hundred problems and planned appropriate corrective actions. Such organizational issues could not have emerged while the technical problems of day-to-day operations predominated. After the session, the managers agreed that "the team-building work doesn't make the job easy, but it does make it possible."

REPRESENTATIVE TEAMS AND COMMITTEES

Committee members represent an interest group or are appointed to contribute particular skills or viewpoints. In part, their function is defensive—to see that their home group is not damaged and, preferably, is enhanced. Additionally, members are expected to contribute to the committee's task, which may be complex and hard to move forward.

Commitment from members is a problem because committees are often temporary. On the other hand, excessive zeal in furthering the committee's business can prejudice the primary job of the individual. It is not an accident that the word "committee" so frequently produces a negative emotional reaction. Committees can be ponderous, ineffective, and maddening; yet effective committees are necessary to coordinate areas of common interest.

One remedy is to develop a committee as a temporary team that resolves the issues blocking its progress and works effectively towards mutually accepted and explicit goals. Here, team-building techniques are invaluable, and individuals develop their competence at being useful members in each group they join.

WORK GROUPS

Since the importance of a team approach in the workplace has been recognized, whole theories of motivation have developed to try to counter the indifference and lack of care that infects many production and service units.

One solution is to use a team concept at the supervisory level. This stresses participation and more workplace democracy, with the overall aim of channeling more of the creative energy of people towards benefiting the organization rather than blocking its progress. The supervisor's role can evolve into that of a team leader, whose function is to facilitate the working of the team rather than to direct it.

There is so much to be said about practical team building at the workplace, that this book is only a starting point.

MANAGEMENT DEVELOPMENT SPECIALISTS

Those involved in developing the management resource in organizations are constantly seeking ways to broaden ideas, develop useful skills, and encourage an assertive, positive approach to management. Management-development specialists can find many useful ideas and techniques in this book. It combines the insights from current research findings with concrete methods for the manager to apply in day-to-day working life. The team-building approach often receives little resistance from managers because they can readily see that it has the potential to help them directly in their jobs.

Management-development specialists can develop themselves as trainers in team-building methods and as internal advisors to managers who are applying team-building techniques with their own teams. This strengthens the specialists' role, gives practical relevance to their work, and gives a coherent, yet flexible, framework to guide management development.

We have seen team-building "take off" in large organizations, focusing the developing of management skills and giving new vitality to personnel and management-development advisors. Unlike more mechanistic approaches to development, the team-building approach rapidly becomes "owned" by managers who fuel further development from their own energy and initiative.

HOW TO START TEAM BUILDING

Little change happens in a group unless someone makes a strong intervention. Most team members become habitualized to their group ailments, although the more adventurous find back-door ways to get things done. So, things go on, with people sometimes coming near to taking an initiative, but drawing back, fearful of exposing an unprotected head.

Team building needs a midwife—one person, or a small corps, who will fuel the team-building process with energy and insight. The catalyst may be a manager, a team member, a company specialist, or an external change agent. (Suggestions on whether or not to select a professional guide are offered in the next chapter.)

One thing is clear from the outset: team building is a process of development and change. Those involved need to have a personal theory of how to accomplish change effectively. This is especially relevant for the person serving as the catalyst.

The term *a theory of change* may create unwarranted tension in people who fear they will have to absorb the contents of bulky tomes with titles like *A Technical Sociopathology of Organizational Dynamics.* Not true. The most valuable data is from your own experience— information that has been reflected over and tested out in your own environment. Your personal theory of change needs to be expressed in terms that you and your colleagues really understand. As you read the next few pages, think through your own approach, clarify the elements, and begin to build your personal theory.

The Change for Alfred

The process of change can be very different for different people. One example is Alfred, a manager we know well. At thirty years of age, Alfred achieved a rapid promotion. He was selected to head a small team that was to develop a promising new market. But after a few months, his immediate staff was vehement in its criticism of his performance. They claimed that, protected by a well-groomed secretary, he brooded in his satinwood office, dictating notes to his staff, and asking for endless jobs to be accomplished at once.

Alfred's notes, impeccably typed and grammatically perfect, flowed on to his subordinates' desks, followed shortly by pointed enquiries as to why the myriad of tasks had not been accomplished. His staff said that Alfred presented himself in a clipped, precise manner that defined the world in terms he could understand but excluded the viewpoints of everyone else. Alfred was aware of his difficulties, but he reacted by becoming more involved in detail and trying to intensify his image as a dynamic, cavalier, young manager.

After a colleague suggested that Alfred try to have an open discussion with his team, a team-development session was carefully planned. Alfred and his group discussed many of the issues very openly. When the private views of the team became public, they shocked Alfred.

Seeking explanation, Alfred talked about his background. He was a scientist who had spent his youth learning obscure facts about protons and anti-matter particles. The scientific method had been his discipline and lonely study had been his means of accomplishment. This method of work became habitual; it led to a good degree and with slight adjustments was sufficient to provide genuine achievement in market research.

In the team-building session, Alfred realized that he was continuing to use acquired attitudes that were appropriate in a science laboratory but were infuriating and ineffective in an executive function. For Alfred, professional development meant learning to share doubts, possibilities, and decisions with others and to deal with the emotional as well as the intellectual issues in his group.

A Different Change for David

David was the manager of a group of construction planners. He was amiable, considerate, diligent, and involved with his team's problems. Yet this was not a happy team. It was ineffective and the members' incapacity to work together was a standing joke. Projects had slow and painful births and wallowed through their successive stages. Somehow the team avoided humiliation by a frenzied burst of emergency repair at the eleventh hour.

At first, this process of indulgence followed by a hysterical reaction was fun, but it so disturbed their digestion and family life that group members became increasingly frustrated. All expressions of discontent were openly expressed and seriously considered. Yet nothing was done because the group collectively had poor decision-making skills. David had absorbed so many books on participative management that he felt uncomfortable about personally taking the decision-making role. His concern with encouraging ideas and maintaining close group relationships was pursued at the expense of clear planning and effective utilization of resources.

For David the change came through learning about group problem solving. He studied his work methods and learned to recognize the points where his team was getting stuck. The group gained insight into its collective responsibility for effective teamwork and began to consciously set aside time to review its performance. This practice became a tradition and probably accounted for the major part of the qualitative improvement noticed within David's group in succeeding months.

The Process of Change

The changes that Alfred and David made were basically new personal decisions taken after they had seen themselves and their options more clearly. Each of them went through the following process of change:

- The individual felt a genuine need to behave in a different way;
- Feedback from the group enabled the person to see himself as an outsider might;
- New insights, experiences, and behaviors were examined and tried experimentally;
- New ways of functioning were arrived at and implemented.

It is often said that practice makes perfect. But it is more accurate to say that while practice does not necessarily make perfect, it certainly makes permanent. Behaviors provoke reactions that justify attitudes that, in turn, stimulate repeat behavior. This cycle is repeated frequently and will only be changed by a definite decision. This process can be diagramed as shown in Figure 2.

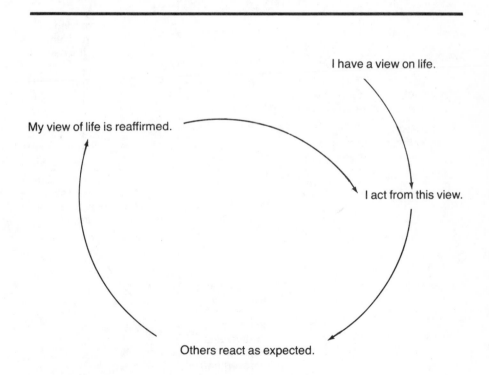

Figure 2. Behavioral cycle

HOW TO MANAGE THE TEAM-BUILDING PROCESS

Steps in Managing Change

There is no system that can replace your own observation of what is happening here-and-now in your world. However, a step-by-step approach to change can help a team to work methodically and prevent the omission of important stages. Practical observation suggests five steps that are important in managing change (see Figure 3).

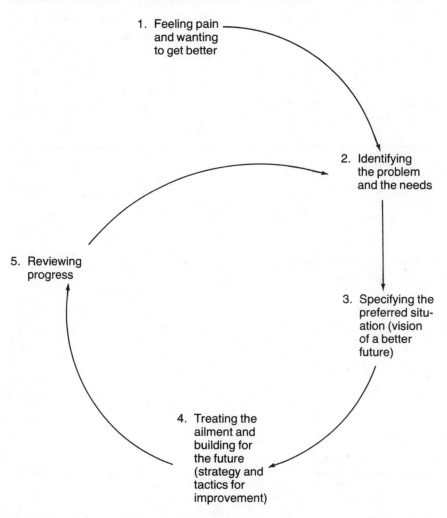

Figure 3. Steps in managing change

STEP 1. WANTING TO FEEL BETTER

Change is never energized from complacency and comfort. Effective change begins with the realization that all is not well or that hazards lurk ahead. At this initial stage, feelings play an important part because the need for change must be felt by those individuals whose opinion carries weight in the organization.

STEP 2. IDENTIFYING THE PROBLEM AND THE NEEDS

Sometimes problems can be difficult for a manager to identify. A manager trying to diagnose a problem can be likened to a television technician trying to repair an intermittent fault. Although the fault cannot be traced until the set goes wrong, the television behaves impeccably while the technician is watching. Because of this difficulty in observing symptoms, a superficial assessment is often made that fails to identify the causes of problems.

A technical analysis of problems needs to be supplemented by an emotional recognition of their importance. Techniques already exist for analyzing the nature of organizational health, but these need to be warily applied lest they run counter to the traditions of the community.

STEP 3. SPECIFYING THE PREFERRED SITUATION

Managing organizational and team changes has much in common with undertaking a journey; it is important to be as clear as possible about where you wish to go.

If you can visualize the changes you wish to see and the hazards that may block you, then you stand a better chance of persevering and achieving. One way of doing this is to project your imagination forward and ask the question, "What do I want to see happening with this team in one year?"

Most people respond to this question by censoring their visualization with practical difficulties. However, at this stage it helps to ignore the practical limitations; they often are in one's head rather than in the reality of the situation. Concentrating on what you wish to see happen will help you build a vision of the future. Others in your team also should clarify their images and then you all can explore common ground.

STEP 4. TREATING THE AILMENTS AND BUILDING FOR THE FUTURE

After the team's vision of the future has been clarified, it should be worked on until it can be expressed in terms of objectives. This is important because visions can be slippery and insubstantial. The products of imagination need to be captured and solidified or, like hobgoblins and ghosts, they will vanish with the dawn.

Once objectives are stated, strategy and tactics can be approached. There are many treatments for team and organizational ailments and not all can be administered at once. An appropriate treatment is one that is affordable and effective.

STEP 5. REVIEWING PROGRESS

Habits and traditions become etched into the fabric of an organization like crusader crosses cut in the desert cliffs. Because it is so easy to slip back and lose impetus or direction, change efforts need to be monitored. Progress can be carefully reviewed by using mechanisms such as a regular meeting, clearly defined responsibilities, open discussion, and outside people who act as mirrors reflecting the group's behavior. These tools for monitoring are not special techniques. Team building can gain much from the same disciplines that managers use in other areas, since similar standards of professionalism are required. Good technical project managers know how to monitor their group's pulse.

Managing the Team-Building Process

OPEN EXCHANGE

All team members should be aware that the team-building process increases the scope of open exchange and, consequently, critical comments or negative feelings may come to the surface. One manager described it as "lifting the stones and letting the nasties crawl out." Team building does not create "nasties," but it does give them a voice to express themselves.

Team building encourages members toward a deeper level of disclosure. If people find that this results in humbug or repression, their worst fears will be confirmed and the team-building process would take a backward step. On the other hand, once a problem is expressed, the team has an opportunity to deal with it creatively. It is vital at this time that the issue be constructively processed.

The team-building process can surface profound issues of concern and dissatisfaction. On such occasions, each person is vulnerable, but the most vulnerable person is the team leader, who has to cope with more group comment than anyone else. Therefore, the team leader is also the person who needs to be most conscious of the process to be used and the probable outcomes of that process. It is important that the leader have a clear understanding of the values that underlie team building, the techniques that should be used, and what will be required of him.

The people who seem to respond best to team-building approaches are managers who practice openness in their relationships with others and who want to get things done. They are looking for a vehicle to manage change more effectively, and they can use team building for this purpose.

AVOIDING BLOWUPS

Usually team-building sessions are interesting and constructive. *Occasionally* they become tedious and dull while the team works through labyrinths of system or strategy. *Rarely* team-building events can blow up with uncomfortable or hurtful incidents.

If group difficulties and blowups are handled with care, they provide a potential for significant progress. The following guidelines can help you to use these team-building materials successfully. However, if things still go wrong, it is best to deal with the incident in an open and straightforward manner and help the team to thoroughly talk through the situation.

1. *Voluntary Involvement.* Ensure that each person not only knows (in outline) what is to happen, but also has freely agreed to be involved in the session. A project always should be discussed before proceeding with it.

2. *Adequate Discussion Time.* When the team undertakes a project, allow sufficient time for all members to express themselves and for the team to consider their reactions. Avoid leaving issues only partially discussed.

3. *Appropriate Sequence.* Begin a project with more impersonal assignments and deepen the members' experience by manageable steps.

4. *Careful Preparation.* All the projects should be set up with care to ensure that the facilities are comfortable and private and the required materials are provided. There is more assurance of effective preparation if one person acts as the organizer/administrator.

5. *Relevant Choices.* Each team has its own history and style. Since some projects work superbly in one team but fail in another, the choice of suitable approaches is crucial. The team itself, is the best arbiter and needs to spend time designing its own program of change.

6. *Avoid Undue Threat.* Any activity that threatens an individual can hurt or provoke aggression. Therefore, projects that could be seen as threatening are acceptable only if they are skillfully undertaken with constructive intentions. In this case, the only judge can be the team itself. Before a team undertakes a project that could bring out hidden information, it is essential that all members know the likely course of events and voluntarily agree to participate.

7. *Work Through Conflicts and Difficulties.* Because difficult situations require thorough resolution, every effort should be made to avoid leaving a program unfinished. It is better to get perspectives and guidance from outside resources than to flounder. If you are at all uncertain about your capacity to conduct a program, find an experienced helper and enlist his or her aid. Trained team-building advisors can help to unblock a group and aid in its progress.

RESOURCES

After the team members accept the idea of team building, they should begin to work at it. But this involves more than a commitment of intent, resources will be required, primarily time and money.

Time

The chief resource needed for team-building is time—time for experiencing, giving and receiving feedback, learning, skill development, and thinking through all the factors influencing the team. Some of this time should be found from the normal working day because it is important that new practices are absorbed into the team's way of life. It is also likely that the team members will need to take time away from the working environment and spend several days working together on team building.

Many teams find that a weekend offers the only opportunity for members to work together in an uninterrupted session. An advantage of residential sessions is exemplified by the members of one group who met at a hotel. After working through a full day's agenda, the members adjourned to the bar. They talked about boats, children, and machines until two in the morning. Then one person suggested, "Why don't we carry on the session with each person saying how he sees the others." There followed one of the frankest interchanges imaginable, which ended two hours later with the group saying that this had been the most valuable part of the session.

Such in-depth exchanges are difficult to engineer in working hours, so a commitment to off-site meetings will probably be necessary. Mixing informality and concentrated working sessions can move a team forward rapidly.

Money

The only other resource required for team building is money. Team building can be undertaken cheaply if those concerned are prepared to put themselves out. Organizations can imaginatively adapt team-building techniques so that little direct expenditure is required. However, it often speeds the process if money is spent on getting the team-building activities moving. The principal expenses are for off-site meetings, especially if residential, and for the services of a specialist who will act as a catalyst to help the group progress.

Specialists in team building are usually trained in the behavioral sciences and their job is to help the group diagnose its ills and resolve problems. Their skills and experience give confidence and pace to the process, but they can only help the process to move. The actual work should be undertaken by the team members themselves. The notion that every manager should have the capacity to develop effective teams has much to commend it.

WHO IS IN THE TEAM?

When you begin a process of team building, it becomes necessary to draw a boundary around a group of people and decide who is *in* and who is *out*. Sometimes this is straightforward. For example, a team might be defined as all managers at the Newark factory or all the technicians responsible for module B of the Lion project.

On the other hand, defining the membership of the team can become a fuzzy and blurred issue. We form and reform into different groupings as the task changes and personal relationships develop. As a new person's contribution becomes significant and previously important people draw back, boundaries become fluid.

Deciding the membership of the group may be a sensitive political decision. Since status may well be affected by membership, pride is at stake. There is no simple mechanical formula for drawing the boundary line in each case. However, we have found it helpful to consider three levels of membership.

Core Team Members. Their contribution is necessary over an extended period, and significant reorganization would be necessary should they withdraw.

Supportive Team Members. Their contribution aids the team to do its work effectively. They do not greatly assist tasks to be performed or spark creative effort. Rather, their contribution is to ease, support, and provide assistance, raw materials, or information.

Temporary Team Members. Their contribution is specific and time-bound. It may be that a particular assignment requires skills absent from the team. An outside person can them become a temporary team member while this special contribution is required. The person then withdraws and ceases to be a team member.

With these three levels of team membership carefully distinguished, it becomes possible to consider each person in relation to his function within the team and clarify his position. In cases where this presents difficulties, we have found it helpful to discuss the issue with the person concerned and members of the core team.

OBJECTIVES

Team building can be a rather obscure and confusing technique to many managers. It helps to have a written statement of preliminary objectives—objectives that are checked at an early point with the team as a whole. (Examples of statements of objectives developed for team building are included later in the book.) One objective for many teams is the development of a common vision of where the group is going. This includes an assessment of the kinds of forces impacting on the group and the shape of things to come. Here, tools for analyzing and thinking through problems and situations are needed. Management groups may lack skill in collecting and displaying data in a form that can be used effectively in making decisions. In that case, we suggest that the group rigorously follow the activity guidelines suggested in this book.

It is common for issues to be raised in team-building sessions that are too deep for immediate assessment or for which further data is required. One of the important outcomes of a team-building session is identification of the mechanisms with which the group will continue to work unresolved issues. These problems should be worked on, clarified, and solved as part of the normal working process of that team. Some objectives will deal with task, some with organization, and some with the group processes.

ORGANIZATION-WIDE DEVELOPMENT

If you are working on team building as part of a program of change stretching across an entire organization, our flexible method can be used as the main plank of such a program. Our method does not suggest a mechanistic sequence of development, which so many managers find artificial and foreign. Rather, we provide tools to work teams and depend on the teams to use creatively what makes sense to them.

It is true that "organization-wide problems require organization-wide solutions." However, large programs of organizational change often resemble military campaigns in hostile terrain, requiring extensive reserves of trained troops. Unfortunately, the grand projects frequently fail and become a sour recollection of a lost opportunity.

Although it is almost impossible for any outside body to energize a large organization and keep it moving, it is possible to spark off the latent energy locked within and channel its expression. If organization-wide development is of special interest to you, it is important to have professional help before making a major commitment. (Information on choosing professional help is provided in the next chapter.)

THE EFFECTS OF CHANGES

Up to a point, a group is capable of remaining effective despite changes in its membership. An effective team will have a method for introducing new people and giving them the repertoire of skills, knowledge, and attitudes that are required to do an effective job. To some extent, a team is capable of sustaining its learning and development despite changes in numerical membership. However, rapid changes of membership put a special stress on the capacity of the team. In particular, it is well known that a change of team manager has profound effects.

The senior group in a large food factory prided themselves on being ahead of the pack. They used the most advanced techniques available for production control, manufacturing, and personnel development. Then the senior group decided to use team-building techniques on themselves. After a number of sessions were held, the members became closer and more competent. They went out of their way to keep each other informed and, almost to the point of compulsion, planned joint projects with their own blend of creativity, order, and energy. The site manager was delighted, saying "This team building has affected us more fundamentally than anything else we've tried."

Several months later the situation in the factory had changed. The site manager put it this way, "Yes, the team building worked, but it worked too well. We put a lot of extra effort into our senior group and this left the next level down feeling more isolated and out of things."

Different components in a system are interdependent. As we change one, so other parts are affected. If one team is built at the expense of others, it can provoke a chain of disorders. One change, quite unintentionally, sparks off others. It is impossible to forecast all the effects of change and requiring absolute certainty before venturing on a new project is a recipe for impotence. However, it is necessary and wise to look ahead and try to spot the potential dangers.

The Team-Development Consultant

This is a "do-it-yourself" manual. We have designed it so that working teams will be able to use it without external dependency. However, there are some circumstances in which teams do need external help in working on their own development. This chapter provides practical help in addressing the following issues concerning choosing and working with a consultant:

- When to use a consultant.
- What consultants can contribute.
- What are the qualities and characteristics of a good team-development consultant?
- Where to find consultants.
- How to choose a suitable consultant.
- The stages of working with a consultant.

WHEN TO USE A CONSULTANT

A consultant can help with a number of problems confronted by a team that is just beginning to consider its own development. Initially, there is the natural apprehension of the team's leaders and members in setting out on an uncharted course. Team managers may feel particularly exposed, especially if they suspect that "nasties" may lurk beneath the surface. Some team members also may feel rather apprehensive about exposing themselves to a new and unknown process.

As their skills develop, teams usually become adept at recognizing their own process problems. But at first, people may be too engrossed in what they are doing to be able to stand back and see what is going on; they can use the perspective of an external agent. And while a team is developing, problems and issues may arise that are particularly difficult or sensitive; these call for the skills of a consultant.

As a team matures, it normally is developing the ability to handle its own problems and the need for external help either is diminishing or is no longer necessary. Later, mature and effective teams may want to spend time with a trusted consultant once or twice a year, just to get another perspective on how things are going.

Lastly, a consultant who is known in the wider organization can help in handling intergroup relationships.

Summary: When To Use a Consultant

- To help start a team-development process.
- When team managers and members do not have the skills at the same time to manage and take part in team-development activities.
- When there are difficult or sensitive issues to be worked through.
- When team members feel that they are too involved in issues to be able to stand back and see what is going on.
- To give impartial feedback on team performance and problems.
- To help a team review progress at intervals.
- When intergroup problems arise, which are difficult for the team to handle alone.

WHAT CONSULTANTS CAN CONTRIBUTE

A consultant cannot make a team effective; teams do that for themselves. There also is no way in which a consultant can do the work of the team. But a consultant can assist a group in many different ways.

Sometimes an organization simply needs someone who possesses expert knowledge not contained in the organization. Once the knowledge is transferred, there is no need for the consultant, who then is paid and leaves. At other times, there are people who possess skills that are beyond the capacity of anybody in the organization. A good example of this are the expert firefighters who put out oil-rig fires.

Team-development consultancy is different from the two other kinds just mentioned. It is not the *content* of the team's work that is being worked on, but the *process* by which members of the team work together. This distinction between *content* and *process* is vital.

A team-development consultant is concerned with helping the team to:

- Identify blockages to effective working.
- Diagnose what is going on inside the team and why the blockages exist.
- Recognize, confront, and work through the problems themselves.
- Set team-development objectives, and chart their own progress.

The consultant's major contributions are likely to be:

- Observing what is happening between team members as the team works.

- Serving as a mirror to the team, so that the members have a clear view of their behavior.

- Selecting activities that are appropriate in helping the team improve its performance.

- Giving feedback to the team and its members on how they are doing.

A team-development consultant will not:

- Usurp leadership, but will support the manager and each member.

- Tell the team what is wrong with it; but will help the team to recognize its own problems.

- Make decisions for the team, but will help the team to make its own decisions.

- Get engrossed and involved in the content of the team's work.

- Make the team dependent on his continued presence; but will work to make the team independent of external help.

Good team-development consultants can provide skills in working sensitively with groups of people in a helping and supportive way and also offer their experience in working with the problems of many teams. It is these skills and experiences that the team is buying.

QUALITIES AND CHARACTERISTICS OF A GOOD TEAM-DEVELOPMENT CONSULTANT

We know a brilliant consultant who failed high school, worked as a carpenter for fifteen years, and then by accident became involved in team-development work. Another successful consultant started work as an engineer and, through his church membership, became involved in social work and then team development. Another colleague has a degree in psychology and a Ph.D. based on psychotherapy research. One of the worst failures we have encountered in consultancy has a degree in sociology and long experience in social work, clinical psychology, and research. Our conclusion is that a string of academic qualifications is no guarantee that a consultant is good.

Distilling the characteristics of effective consultants is difficult because of the wide diversity of backgrounds and experience shared by those we have known, but here is our best attempt.

An effective consultant:

1. Is a person who has self-knowledge, gained from a breadth and depth of personal experience. This knowledge cannot be developed from text books or academic education. It comes, rather, from working extensively with other people and working through their own personal values. A consultant is likely to manifest these characteristics through behaviors such as:

- Listening actively.
- Valuing others as people.
- Taking people as they are.
- Having space and time for working with others.
- Abstaining from personal crusading and dogmatic views.
- Clarifying his personal values.
- Confronting people and issues positively.
- Reflecting problems to people in a helpful way.

2. Has a foundation of practical theory. This does not mean an ability to regurgitate other people's theories, impressive though this may seem. It does mean that the individual is able to draw on research and theory in a relevant way to guide his work.

3. Is open and realistic. Some consultants will promise the world. Others are subtle manipulators who attempt to con or even threaten others into changed behaviors. A good consultant will be open in giving feedback to others and will be quite explicit about his own values. Importantly, he also will develop a clear "contract" at the beginning of a job, which will define the expectations and responsibilities of both client and consultant.

4. Can work with the team on the here and now issues, but also encourage the members to visualize ways of improving for the future. However, beware the consultant who lives always in the future, especially where results are concerned.

WHERE TO FIND CONSULTANTS?

When an organization has no need for a consultant, it may be assailed by publicity material promising dramatic consulting results in every field conceivable — from Accounting to Zen meditation.

Paradoxically, when there is a specific need, then finding the right consultant may become a challenge. Sometimes it seems as though all the good consultants have migrated to greener fields, are booked for the next year, or were last heard of heading for the desert to write a book.

However, the right consultant can be found somewhere—in business schools, other centers of management education, large and small consultancy firms, inside other companies, and in independent practice. Consultants work under many different titles with the commonest being: group facilitator, group-training specialist, team-development agent, and personal-skills specialist.

The very best way to find the right *individual* to meet your needs is by personal recommendation from people who have had good experiences. To do this, first check with companies or other organizations who have done some work in group training or team development.

A second approach is asking a local business school to recommend someone. If this fails to produce results, find a management publication containing material relevant to your interests. Then contact the publisher or the author to see if they know of any suitable people. If you still have no success, try the larger consultant firms that specialize in personal skills and group training, or contact the associations of consultants and management associations that exist in most countries.

A word of warning: when approaching large institutions or consultancies, remember that you are going to work with an individual person, not the institution, so check on the person who will be doing the work.

As a last resort, define your need, write it on a plain postcard, and send it to the authors, who will try to be of help.

HOW TO CHOOSE A SUITABLE CONSULTANT

It is wise, first, to check out the work of a prospective consultant and look for relevance to your needs and standards of quality. Any consultant worth his salt will be pleased to refer you to past clients; if necessary, visit them.

A second tactic is talking with several consultants and choosing one of them. Discuss your problems with each consultant and work through whatever strategy is proposed. Does it feel right? Realistic? Not too slick?

In working these issues with you, the consultants should be showing some of the behavioral skills that will be manifest in their work. Reject a consultant such as the one who totally disrupted a whole office by his pushy and pompous telephone behavior. Finally, when he reached the manager and announced that he was a "specialist in human relations," the manager, having heard the effects of the man's behavior, just said, "I don't believe you!" and hung up.

Another criterion is whether you feel any personal warmth, trust, and understanding developing. This is critical because a team-development consultant will be working in potentially intimate contact with a team and each one of its members. The initial exploration of problems with a team manager and the team (done before any commitment to work is made) should be deep enough to enable the team to develop a personal feeling of whether it would feel good about working with the consultant.

Something to check as part of the initial "contract" with a consultant is whether he will devote sufficient time and energy to service your needs.

Finally, can you afford the consultant? Consultancy is not cheap, but a good consultant can make all the difference to the success of your team's development.

THE STAGES OF WORKING WITH A CONSULTANT

Effective management of the introduction of a consultant to your team or organization will reduce the risks of a bad experience. The process could include the following steps:

1. Review and identify the group's needs. What issues and problems does the team feel it has? Can these be handled internally or should they be dealt with by somebody in the wider organization? Here the Team-Review Questionnaire can be of great use.

2. Obtain consensus from the team concerning the need for an external consultant. If there is a general feeling that skilled outside help is necessary, then move to the next step.

3. Scan the environment to identify a number of suitable consultants and have them meet other team members.

4. Select the most appropriate consultant.

5. Develop a "contract" with the consultant. This is not so much a formal written document as a mutual understanding that covers the following:

   - The initial diagnosis of the problems to be worked on.
   - The method of working on these problems.
   - How much further diagnosis is required, and how this will be done.
   - The relationship between the consultant and team members (especially the team manager).
   - What kind of role the consultant normally likes to play.
   - The design of initial activities.
   - How progress will be reviewed.
   - How success will be judged.
   - When work will start.

- The time scale over which work will be carried out.
- The broad amount of consultancy time required.
- How much this will cost, and how the consultant will be paid.

6. Complete the initial diagnostic work and plan the initial activities. As much as possible, this should be done with and accepted by the whole team.

7. Start work. Review.

8. Identify how and broadly when the consultant will begin to withdraw from the team. A good consultant's major aim will be to bring the team to a position in which it is strong enough to handle its own development without external help. Make sure this issue is raised with the consultant.

At some stage in a team's growth, an outsider may be an essential agent to help unblock problems. But, in the end, the health and effectiveness of any team must be assessed by the team itself.

2

The Team-Review
Questionnaire

The foundations have been laid, benefits listed, caveats sounded, and processes explained. Now the time has come to delve and search—to focus on your team. To do this, we invite you to complete the Team-Review Questionnaire in relation to a particular team.

Before undertaking the questionnaire, decide precisely who you are assessing and ensure that all those involved freely agree to this as a team assignment.

ADMINISTERING THE TEAM-REVIEW QUESTIONNAIRE

Purpose

I. To help a work team address its strengths and weaknesses.

II. To determine whether the group has the desire and the energy to begin a team-building program.

III. To help a team understand the characteristics of effective team-work.

Time

A minimum of two hours.

Materials

I. A copy of the Team-Review Questionnaire, the Team-Review Questionnaire Answer Sheet, the Team-Review Questionnaire Interpretation Sheet, and a pencil for each participant. (As explained on the copyright page, our publisher permits you to freely copy these sheets, but for internal and nonprofit use only.)

II. Blank paper for each participant.

III. A large pad of paper to use as a blank flip chart (newsprint is handy), masking tape, and a felt-tipped marking pen, or a chalkboard and chalk.

Physical Arrangement

A quiet room where team members can sit and write comfortably.

Method

I. One person in the team, often the manager, takes an hour prior to the meeting to become familiar with the method described in "Analysing the Team-Review Questionnaire," which follows the questionnaire. This person acts as coordinator and discussion leader for the session.

II. The session begins with a brief explanation by the coordinator about the process the team is about to undertake. He emphasizes that voluntary involvement is essential and invites people to express their concerns. Only if there is full agreement should the questionnaire materials be distributed and the activity continue. (Ten minutes.)

III. Team members complete the questionnaire, including the interpretation sheet. (Twenty minutes.)

IV. Using the information given in "Analyzing the Team-Review Questionnaire," the coordinator guides the team in charting the reactions. (Fifteen minutes.)

V. Now comes the most significant part of the activity. The coordinator introduces a discussion of the results, and the team members discuss the following questions for approximately twenty minutes each.

1. How valid are the Team-Review Questionnaire results?

2. What are the significant strengths and weaknesses of the team?

3. What resources are we prepared to devote to strengthening our team and working through blocks?

It is important to be very specific about the last question. One way of measuring the team's commitment is to allocate money to the project. If a team is willing to spend scarce resources on self-development, then it is clearly committed and action is more likely to follow.

VI. When the discussion has been concluded, the team as a whole should make the decision whether to proceed with team building. Sometimes it is useful to allow a few days for reflection before the final decision is made. Once this is done, if the team wishes to proceed, it can progress through this book experimenting, adapting, and learning from its experience.

THE TEAM-REVIEW QUESTIONNAIRE

Instructions

PART 1

Write in the following space a precise definition of the team under review. Either write the names of all those included or a designation that is unmistakable.

```
The team under review is




```

PART 2

You will find 108 statements listed below. Think about each statement in relation to the identified team. Use the Team-Review Questionnaire Answer Sheet to respond to the statements. If you feel that a statement is broadly true, mark an X on the appropriate number in the answer sheet grid. If you feel that a statement is not broadly true, then leave that number blank.

Work methodically through the questionnaire, answering each question. There may be times when you find it difficult to answer a particular question but come to the best answer you can. It might be useful to note in the margin the numbers of these difficult questions.

Remember that the quality of the result is directly related to your own openness when answering the questions. This is not meant to be a scientific survey, but rather it serves as a tool to provoke thought and discussion.

1. The team's manager and members spend little time in clarifying what they expect and need from one another.

2. The work of the team would improve if members upgraded their technical qualifications.

3. Most of the members feel that the aims of the team are hardly worthwhile.

4. People in this team often are not really frank and open with each other.

5. The objectives of our team are not really clear.

6. Team members are unsure about the team's contribution to the wider organization.

7. We rarely achieve much progress in team meetings.

8. The objectives of some individual team members do not gel with those of other members.

9. When team members are criticized, they often feel that they have lost face.

10. New members often are just left to find their own place in the team.

11. Not many new ideas are generated by the team.

12. Conflicts between our team and other groups are quite common.

13. The team manager rarely tolerates leadership efforts by other team members.

14. Some team members are unable to handle the current requirements of their work.

15. Team members are not really committed to the success of the team.

16. In group discussion, team members often hide their real motives.

17. In practice, the team rarely achieves its objectives.

18. Our team's contribution is not clearly understood by other parts of the organization.

19. When the team is having a meeting, we do not listen to each other.

20. Team members are uncertain about their individual roles in relation to the team.

21. Members often restrain their critical remarks to avoid "rocking the boat."

22. The potential of some team members is not being developed.

23. Team members are wary about suggesting new ideas.

24. Our team does not have constructive relationships with some of the other teams within the organization.

25. Team members are uncertain where they stand with the team manager.

26. Our mix of skills is inappropriate to the work we are doing.

27. I do not feel a strong sense of belonging to the team.

28. It would be helpful if the team could have "clear-the-air" sessions more often.

29. In practice, low levels of achievement are accepted.

30. If the team were disbanded, the organization would not feel the loss.

31. The team meetings often seem to lack a methodical approach.

32. There is no regular review of individual objectives and priorities.

33. The team is not good at learning from its mistakes.

34. Team members tend not to show initiative in keeping up-to-date or in developing themselves.

35. We have the reputation of being stick-in-the-muds.

36. The team does not respond sufficiently to the needs of other teams in the organization.

37. The team manager gets little information about how the team sees his performance.

38. People outside the team consider us as unqualified to meet work requirements.

39. I am not prepared to put myself out for the team.

40. Important issues often are "swept under the carpet" and not worked through.

41. Individuals are given few incentives to stretch themselves.

42. There is confusion between the work of this team and the work of others.

43. Team members rarely plan or prepare for meetings.

44. If team members are missing, their work just does not get done.

45. Attempts to review events critically are seen as negative and harmful.

46. Little time and effort is spent on individual development and training.

47. This team seldom innovates anything.

48. We do not actively seek to develop our working relationships with other teams.

49. The team would get better quality decisions if the team members took the initiative.

50. The team's total level of ability is too low.

51. Some team members find it difficult to commit themselves to doing the job well.

52. There is too much stress placed on conformity.

53. Energy is absorbed in unproductive ways and does not go into getting results.

54. The role of our team is not clearly identified within the organization.

55. The team does not set aside time to consider and review how it tackles problems.

56. Much improvement is needed in communication between team members.

57. We would benefit from an impartial assessment of how we work.

58. Most team members have been trained only in their technical discipline.

59. Good ideas seem to get lost.

60. Some significant mistakes would have been avoided if we had better communication with other teams.

61. The team manager often makes decisions without talking them through with the team.

62. We need an input of new knowledge and skills to make the team complete.

63. I wish I could feel more motivated by working in this team.

64. Differences between team members rarely are properly worked through.

65. No time is devoted to questioning whether our efforts have been worthwhile.

66. We do not have an adequate way to establish our team's objectives and strategy.

67. We often seem to get bogged down when a difficult problem is being discussed in team meetings.

68. The team does not have adequate administrative resources and procedures.

69. We lack the skills to review our effectiveness constructively.

70. The team does not take steps to develop its members.

71. New ideas from outside the team seldom are accepted.

72. In this organization, teams and departments tend to compete rather than collaborate.

73. The team manager does not adapt his style to changing circumstances.

74. New people coming into the team sometimes lack the necessary qualifications.

75. No one is trying hard to make this a winning team.

76. Individuals in this team do not really get to know each other as people.

77. We seem more concerned about giving a good appearance than achieving results.

78. The organization does not use the vision and skills that the team has to offer.

79. We have team meetings, but do not properly examine their purpose.

80. We function in rather a rigid manner and are not sufficiently flexible in using team resources.

81. Performance would improve if constructive criticism were encouraged.

82. Individuals who are retiring or uncertain often are overridden.

83. It would be fair to say that the team has little vision.

84. Some of the other teams/departments seem to have a low opinion of us.

85. The team manager is not sufficiently sensitive to the different needs of each member.

86. Some team members are not adapting to the needs of the team, despite efforts to help them.

87. If a team member gets into difficulties, he usually is left to cope with them by himself.

88. There are cliques and political maneuvering in the team.

89. Nothing that we do could be described as excellent.

90. The team's objectives have not been systematically related to the objectives of the whole organization.

91. Decisions made at meetings are not properly recorded or activated.

92. Team members could collaborate much more if they examined the possibilities of doing so on a person-by-person basis.

93. Little time is spent on reviewing what the team does, how it works, and how to improve it.

94. A person who questions the established practices in the team probably will be smartly put back in place.

95. Only a few members suggest new ideas.

96. We do not get to know the people working in other teams in the organization.

97. I do not know whether our team is adequately represented at higher levels.

98. Some team members need considerable development to do their work effectively.

99. Team members are committed to individual goals at the expense of the team.

100. Disagreements between team members are seldom worked through thoroughly and individual viewpoints are not fully heard.

101. We often fail to finish things satisfactorily.

102. We do not work within clear strategic guidelines.

103. Our meetings do not properly resolve all the issues that should be dealt with.

104. We do not examine how the team spends its time and energy.

105. We make resolutions but, basically, we don't learn from our mistakes.

106. Individuals are not encouraged to go outside the team to widen their personal knowledge and skills.

107. Creative ideas often are not followed through to definite action.

108. If we worked better with other teams, it would help us all to be more effective.

TEAM-REVIEW QUESTIONNAIRE ANSWER SHEET

- Follow the instructions at the beginning of the questionnaire.
- In the grid shown here there are 108 squares, each one numbered to correspond to the statements on the questionnaire.
- If you think a statement is broadly true about your team, mark an *X* through the square. If you feel a statement is not broadly true, then leave the square blank.
- Fill in the top line first, working from left to right; then fill in the second line, etc.
- Be careful to respond to each statement, but mark an asterisk next to the numbers of statements that you find especially significant or difficult to answer. These can be explored later.

Answer Grid

1	2	3	4	5	6	7	8	9	10	11	12
13	14	15	16	17	18	19	20	21	22	23	24
25	26	27	28	29	30	31	32	33	34	35	36
37	38	39	40	41	42	43	44	45	46	47	48
49	50	51	52	53	54	55	56	57	58	59	60
61	62	63	64	65	66	67	68	69	70	71	72
73	74	75	76	77	78	79	80	81	82	83	84
85	86	87	88	89	90	91	92	93	94	95	96
97	98	99	100	101	102	103	104	105	106	107	108

Totals

I	II	III	IV	V	VI	VII	VIII	IX	X	XI	XII

Please do not turn the page until you have completed answering all the questions. When you have responded to all 108 statements, total the number of *X's* in each vertical column, write the total in the space shown at the bottom of the column, then turn to the next page.

TEAM-REVIEW QUESTIONNAIRE INTERPRETATION SHEET

When you have totaled all the *X's* in each of the twelve vertical columns of the Answer Grid, copy these totals next to the appropriate Roman numerals on the chart shown here.

	Your Score	Your Ranking	Team Average	Team Ranking	
I					Inappropriate Leadership
II					Unqualified Membership
III					Insufficient Group Commitment
IV					Unconstructive Climate
V					Low Achievement Orientation
VI					Undeveloped Corporate Role
VII					Ineffective Work Methods
VIII					Inadequate Team Organization
IX					Soft Critiquing
X					Stunted Individual Development
XI					Lack of Creative Capacity
XII					Negative Intergroup Relations

List below the three highest scores for yourself and for the team average.

Personal Highest Scores	Block Title
1.	
2.	
3.	

Team Average Highest Scores	Block Title
1.	
2.	
3.	

The blockages with the highest scores are probably the major issues your team has to face. However, these results need to be verified by discussion and further evaluation.

ANALYZING THE TEAM-REVIEW QUESTIONNAIRE

Now that the questionnaire has been completed, further explanation of the framework of analysis is helpful. Team members usually want to compare and contrast each other's scores directly after the completion of the questionnaire or, if it was completed prior to the meeting, at an early stage in the session. The following procedure quickly brings out key points and provides a reliable bank of reference information. You will need a large newsprint pad, chalkboard, or a similar method of displaying information.

First, find out whether each team member is willing to share his scores. Depending on the decision of the team, scores may be reported anonymously or each member may announce his scores. These scores are posted on a master chart and they are totaled both horizontally and vertically. A sample master chart for a team of five is shown here. Draw up a similar chart, with the appropriate number of columns, for your team.

Blockage	Mary	Tom	Harry	Sandra	Joe	Totals	Priority
I							
II							
III							
IV							
V							
VI							
VII							
VIII							
IX							
X							
XI							
XIII							
TOTALS							

Scoring Chart for the Team-Review Questionnaire

The vertical score in the scoring chart is a personal assessment. Individual variations may be due to differences in the criteria used to complete the questionnaire or to differences in perception. In either event, they are worthy of discussion.

The horizontal scores on the scoring chart are of special significance because they show the team's areas of strength and its needs for development as identified by the members. Low totals indicate strong areas that only require reinforcement, whereas high totals indicate probable blockage areas that require attention to be cleared.

The idea of strengths and blocks is vital to understanding our approach to team building. Our understanding of this concept came from investigation of teams working in industry, commerce, education, social welfare, shipping, media production, and military organizations. We tried to analyze the strengths and weaknesses of actual working teams and to evaluate their effectiveness. A theory gradually merged, and we further refined it by testing it on team-building sessions.

It became clear to us that teams do not emerge from the end of a production line like pressed steel components; but rather, if the environment is favorable, they grow like crystals. It is helpful to think of the team process as a series of steps towards maturity. As the team progresses towards maturity it has to overcome problems. If these problems are not faced or resolved, they become what we call *blocks* or *blockages.*

Team blocks inhibit the flow of team energy. When a block is fully cleared it enables positive energy to flow and, in a way, the block becomes a generator. Each team has to find ways of overcoming blocks and transforming them into generators. Twelve blocks can be identified and each hazards team effectiveness. However, each of these twelve blocks can also become strengths and a source of team energy. Seen in this way, the display of the survey results of your team gives much information.

The priority column in the scoring chart further identifies the significance of the blockages to the group. Priority 1 goes to the highest total score (horizontal) for any blockage, continuing through priority 12, which goes to the lowest score. After determining the blockage priorities, draw attention to priorities 1, 2, and 3. These are the areas deserving the most clarification and action in the future.

When the data have been collected and identified, the remainder of the session is devoted to discussing them. Some groups find it helpful to work through one questionnaire and discuss each person's responses to the key questions. The discussion can lead the team in many directions but should be concluded with a summary of key points and a discussion of future possibilities for action.

CASE STUDY

An example of the way one actual team used the Team-Review Questionnaire can sharpen learning at this stage. The team, consisting of six members, was part of the corporate organization of a large group. When the review was done, the team had been in existence for about twelve months. However, team members' length of service to the larger group ranged from thirty years to three months. The function performed by the team was a relatively new one in the large group. Consequently, the team was still in the process of forming, and its mission, strategies, work programs, and relationships were still being explored. This was causing some uncertainty and stress within the team.

The review was initiated by the team manager. One day, at a team meeting, he introduced the questionnaire, explained its purposes, and asked members whether they saw practical value in doing a team review. Some uncertainty was expressed, but a consensus found some use in analyzing and discussing team operations. A time for a review meeting was arranged and the team members took questionnaires away with them to complete individually.

The Review Meeting

The team manager began the scheduled meeting by presenting the objectives of the team review and suggesting that the initial meeting display the results of the questionnaire and briefly discuss their significance. If the results proved to be significant, then a longer off-site meeting could be arranged.

When the team members, including the manager, read off their results, these were displayed on a flip chart, as shown in Figure 4. After the team totals were reviewed, those with the highest numbers were marked with asterisks to show their high priority. The factor of whether the results reflected the members' feelings was checked out, and the team affirmed that they did.

At this stage, one team member observed that it seemed to him that there were two different kinds of issue present. One was concerned with the *organization* and the team's *method of working.* The other was concerned with the *personal feelings* that some members had for each other.

The team discussed the member's observation and accepted it as accurate. Someone suggested that since the first issue could be handled more easily than the second, why not try to work on the first, see how that went, and then decide on how to handle the second? This seemed appropriate, so the team began brainstorming the subjects of

CATEGORY	Colin	Lynne	Jim	Pamela	Mike	Jane	TOTAL
I. Leadership	•	•	•	•	1	3	4
II. Membership	•	4	2	1	2	2	11
III. Commitment	1	•	•	•	•	•	1
IV. Climate	•	4	4	3	3	4	18*
V. Achievement Orientation	•	1	1	1	•	2	5
VI. Corporate Role	2	2	3	4	6	•	17*
VII. Work Methods	•	1	7	3	5	2	18*
VIII. Team Organization	3	5	2	2	4	4	20*
IX. Critiquing	1	3	2	2	2	3	13
X. Individual Development	1	•	•	•	1	2	4
XI. Creative Capacity	•	•	•	1	•	2	3
XII. Intergroup Relations	5	3	•	3	4	3	18*
TOTAL	13	23	21	20	28	27	

Figure 4. Results of a case-study team review

organization and work methods. The following ideas were recorded on the team's flip chart:

ORGANIZATION

• Communication is a problem. People spend much of their time out of the office, are too busy, etc. *Action:* Improve our meetings.
• Our administrative backup organization and resources are inadequate. *Action:* Extend Jane's role to working in an administrative support capacity for the whole team, rather than just Jim.

- We are not clear enough about in-team roles. There is need for more definition and differentiation. *Action:* Work on the roles of Lynne, Pamela, and Colin.
- Priorities and goals need clarification. It has been assumed that everybody was clear about these, and they are not. *Action:* Jim to prepare a short paper on priorities for the next meeting.

MEETINGS

- We need regular meetings every two weeks.
- We should have an agenda.
- Each person will do a one-page resume of what he has done in the previous two weeks.
- Pamela will be responsible for arranging meetings.

OTHER DECISIONS

- Colin and Jim, the team manager, will meet to clarify Colin's role.
- Pamela, Lynne, Mike, and Jim will get together to work on the roles of Lynne and Pamela and their training needs.

The proposed action steps were reviewed and accepted by the team, and work was carried out on them in the next four weeks.

At the first regular meeting, the results were reported and programs were set up to continue work on role clarification and training. At the end of this first meeting, the team agreed to set aside two days for working through in more depth:

1. Interpersonal relationships; and
2. The team's mission in the wider organization.

The team had the one-day, off-site meeting for working on interpersonal relationships. This meeting clarified a number of negative feelings that the team members felt about one of their number.

The process started with an activity that elicited statements of "How I see you, How you see me, I would like you to do more of . . ., I would like you to do less of . . . " By keeping the issues at this level, a number of personal programs were evolved with commitment from individuals to work on their own programs and from the team to meet again in three months to review progress and feelings. Another day was spent reviewing work done by Jim and Mike on the team's mission and priorities.

Three months after the initial team-review meeting, the team met and came to the following conclusions:

- Organization was clearer;
- People had clearer roles that they could handle;
- Communications were better throughout meetings and outside them;
- Openness between members was greater and work on this should continue;
- The whole process of review was well worthwhile and should continue.

We will leave our study of this team at this meeting. If the members want to take their team building further and are willing to devote the required time, then the next step would be to prepare an action plan for a three-month period. It would be convenient at this stage for each team member to have a copy of this book and to have read it before the next session.

At later meetings, all the members are asked to describe activities they feel would most benefit the group. After their assessment of the best course to follow, a three-month action plan is developed. Then review meetings are arranged, probably at two-week intervals, and a team-development program is started.

Once you have started team building, be a little adventurous and enjoy yourself. Experiment with the materials, while allowing time to discuss the results both at the levels of thinking and feeling.

3

Generating
Team Development

Team effectiveness cannot be measured with the precision of a digital watch. Although the Team-Review Questionnaire examines the key aspects of a team's effectiveness, much of the reported information clearly is subjective. Because of the obvious importance of your own standards, this part of the book is concerned with how you can evaluate the effectiveness and maturity level of a team.

Here the book examines the characteristics of an effective and developed team and attempts to set standards and clarify thinking. The expression "good teamwork" can easily become an empty phrase, so we try to avoid being woolly or over-theoretical. Straightforward criteria are needed for judging a team's level of development and for planning a practical program of team building.

In our search for the characteristics of an effective team, we have identified twelve. We call these *generators* because they can release energy and give the team the capacity to achieve. When a generator is not functioning, it stunts a team's growth and inhibits its effectiveness. We call this inhibition a *block* or *blockage.*

This part of the book will help you to make sense of the results of the Team-Review Questionnaire. Each section explains in more depth the survey results. It makes sense, therefore, for you and your team to find the areas identified as blockages for your team and study them in particular. The sections are numbered with Roman numerals matching those in the Team-Review Questionnaire. This reading should increase your insight into the specific problems caused by an identified blockage. Our definition of a developed team is one that possesses the twelve generators to a satisfactory degree.

Each descriptive section begins with a list of the Team-Review questions that apply to the blockage/generator covered in that section.

These help you assess in detail the relevance of that section to your own team. Although there is some overlap of content in each section, the generator/blockages are sufficiently distinct to be identified and worked on separately.

At the end of each descriptive section is a list of relevant activities that will help you explore that particular blockage and transform it into a generator for your team. The numbered activities are found in Part 4 of this book.

AN EFFECTIVE TEAM

A team that is mature and effective has been painstakingly built. Problems have been worked through, relationships deepened, and roles clarified. When successful teams are examined, we find that they have achieved definite progress in the following distinct areas:

1. *Appropriate Leadership.* The team manager has the skills and intention to develop a team approach and allocates time to team-building activities. Management in the team is seen as a shared function. Individuals other than the manager are given the opportunity to exercise leadership when their skills are appropriate to the needs of the team.

2. *Suitable Membership.* Team members are individually qualified and capable of contributing the "mix" of skills and characteristics that provide an appropriate balance.

3. *Commitment to the Team.* Team members feel a sense of individual commitment to the aims and purposes of the team. They are willing to devote personal energy to building the team and supporting other team members. When working outside the team boundaries, the members feel a sense of belonging to and representing the team.

4. *Constructive Climate.* The team has developed a climate in which people feel relaxed, able to be direct and open, and prepared to take risks.

5. *Concern To Achieve.* The team is clear about its objectives, which are felt to be worthwhile. It sets targets of performance that are felt to be stretching but achievable. Energy is mainly devoted to the achievement of results, and team performance is reviewed frequently to see where improvements can be made.

6. *Clear Corporate Role.* The team has contributed to corporate planning and has a distinct and productive role within the overall organization.

7. *Effective Work Methods.* The team has developed lively, systematic, and effective ways to solve problems together.

8. *Well-Organized Team Procedures.* Roles are clearly defined, communication patterns are well developed, and administrative procedures support a team approach.

9. *Critique Without Rancor.* Team and individual errors and weaknesses are examined, without personal attack, to enable the group to learn from its experience.

10. *Well-Developed Individuals.* Team members are deliberately developed and the team can cope with strong individual contributions.

11. *Creative Strength.* The team has the capacity to create new ideas through the interactions of its members. Some innovative risk taking is rewarded, and the team will support new ideas from individual members or from outside. Good ideas are followed through into action.

12. *Positive Intergroup Relations.* Relationships with other teams have been systematically developed to provide open personal contact and identify where joint working may give maximum pay off. There is regular contact and review of joint or collective priorities with other teams. Individuals are encouraged to contact and work with members of other teams.

I. Effective Leadership

REVIEW QUESTIONS

1. The team's manager and members spend little time in clarifying what they expect and need from one another.

13. The team manager rarely tolerates leadership efforts by other team members.

20. Team members are uncertain about their individual roles in relation to the team.

37. The team manager gets little information about how the team sees his performance.

49. The team would get better quality decisions if the members sometimes took the initiative.

61. The team manager often makes decisions without talking them through with the team.

73. The team manager does not adapt his style to changing circumstances.

85. The team manager is not sufficiently sensitive to the different needs of each member.

97. I do not know whether our team is adequately represented at higher levels.

The single most important factor in determining the quality of teamwork is the way in which a group is led. Some managers view leadership as an antiquated and tarnished concept, but we do not concur. However, leadership, like virtue, is hard to identify, and paradoxically, it is most clearly recognized in its absence. A leader who is unwilling to use a team approach, or who lacks the skills to develop this style of management, will squash any initiative to build a team.

All organizations that are in common use have hierarchies and persons selected to be in charge of others. The organizational manager is accountable upwards for the behavior of the people who report to him. Some functions of leadership—answering on behalf of the group and regulating output—are firmly tied to the role. Although the power belonging to the position may be used rarely, it is present and permanent.

The idea of hierarchy is reflected by the language used to describe working roles such as *supervisor* and *subordinate.* Since words are the currency of thoughts, it is easy to assume that managers have a divine right to exercise their authority. Such viewpoints are alien to developing team building.

Clearly, managers do have special responsibilities and functions, but if they want to use a team approach it is important for them to avoid hiding behind the symbols of eminence and the mannerisms of distance.

For the sake of clarity, we refer to this formal head of a team as the *team manager* rather than the *team leader,* because leadership is a broad function that may ebb and flow subject to the task in hand. However, the team manager is recognized by the organization and is vital to the performance of the team both as an energizing and a creative force.

The principles of *clarifying* and *working through* relevant issues are fundamental to a team approach. Teams grow in stature and competence through explicit and clear exploration of issues that affect them. Their differences and problems can become sources of strength if dealt with in an open and effective problem-solving way.

Developing an open approach with teams is an interesting process with wide intellectual appeal. However, it often becomes uncomfortable, perhaps frightening, and many people shy away from it. The role of team management is to make this opening and developmental process happen.

This can be done by setting a personal example, demonstrating an open approach in practice, and allowing others to lead the team sometimes. Work group members are much more concerned with the actual behavior of their manager than with the words he utters. Therefore, personal exposure and willingness to deal with uncomfortable issues are necessary requirements for the team manager. Once the barriers are broken through, the release of energy and greater depth of relationship more than repays the discomfort.

The important distinction between the roles of manager and leader is that the leadership function is not held irrevocably by one person. Well-developed teams with a sensitive knowledge of the strength of their members rearrange their resources to suit the task in hand. Hence, it is quite possible for the leadership of a team to be diffused, with different people coming to the fore in their area of strengths. This healthy process can be blocked by a formal team manager who refuses to relinquish information and control. Paradoxically, a manager often can be of most service to his team by letting go of the organization-given right to decide and execute and by encouraging the people who are best equipped to lead at the time.

In team building, the skills most needed by a formal team manager are: linking together individuals who can contribute, bringing clarity to objectives, building a climate that is both supportive and confronting, ensuring that work methods are satisfying and effective, and setting a discipline within which relevant issues are always explored. These functions are very different from the conventional requirements that a manager should make decisions, exert control, and exercise discipline. The chief difference is that decisions, control, and discipline are seen more as team functions than as an individual's sole prerogative.

Much has been written about management style, but our standpoint is that your style is personal and you are responsible for it. Managers whom we have enjoyed and worked well with have a management style that is:

- Natural to the person;

- Appropriate to the task and the people;

- Open, so that real issues are confronted;

- Affirmative, expressing an optimistic view of human nature.

Successful team managers are skilled at dealing with feelings of people along with the practical methods of effective problem solving.

Managers who have turned us off and sent us looking for other jobs, we describe as:

- Overbearing

- Inconsistent

- Malicious

- Unenergetic

- Stultifying

- Game playing

The words we have chosen are emotive and deprecating, rather than scientific, because that is how it is. Emotions carry a lot of weight in relationships and the personal values and skills of managers are fully relevant.

Teams evolve over time and go through stages of growth. Although teams are more vulnerable to stunted growth and aberrant mutations than a plant in your garden, their growth patterns are detectable and largely predictable. As the team grows and matures, the contribution of the team manager also will change.

In the early phase of team formation, the manager will be very influential in establishing patterns of relationship, which rapidly can become enshrined traditions. To be effective, the team manager should put energy into encouraging members towards more personal under-standing of each other. From deeper relationships emerges trust, which is one index of team maturity.

The effective team manager will demonstrate strongly that issues are worked through to clear resolution. Team members carefully watch the team manager to see whether action matches spoken intentions and how open they can be without provoking wrath or scorn. Only experi-ence enables an appropriate climate to form and the skills and contri-butions required of the team manager are:

- Being energetic;
- Using team-development skills;
- Being open and encouraging openness;
- Aiding personal relationships;
- Having consistent values and practice.

Later in the team's development towards maturity, the leadership function becomes more widely spread throughout the team. Because of its growing maturity, the group is increasingly capable of handling complex problems. Resourcefulness grows in individuals and the team develops substantial attention and creativity. The team manager be-comes increasingly concerned with activities outside the boundaries of the immediate group.

When well developed, a team can survive upheaval and is capable of considerable innovation in its leadership process. However, this is not easily achieved. Much learning, insight, and effort must go into the clarifying and working through that transforms a collection of individ-uals into an effective team. The primary concern of the team manager is aiding this process to happen.

SUGGESTED ACTIVITIES FOR BLOCKAGE/GENERATOR I: EFFECTIVE LEADERSHIP

Activity Number & Title

   7. Defining Leadership Style
   8. The Best Leaders I Have Known
   9. Who Performs the Leadership Functions
   10. Negotiating the Team Manager's Role

II. Suitable Team Membership

REVIEW QUESTIONS

2. The work of the team would improve if members upgraded their technical qualifications.

14. Some team members are unable to handle the current requirements of their work.

26. Our mix of skills is inappropriate to the work we are doing.

38. People outside the team consider us unqualified to meet work requirements.

50. The team's total level of ability is too low.

62. We need an input of new knowledge and skills to make the team complete.

74. New people coming into the team sometimes lack the necessary qualifications.

86. Some team members are not adapting to the needs of the team, despite efforts to help them.

98. Some team members need considerable development to do their work effectively.

Despite the effective training of management and social skills and the excellence of much personal-development work, exceptional change in people is rarely encountered. This is not to say that training is irrelevant or impotent. The expression "You can't make a silk purse out of a sow's ear" regretably often is true in relation to people.

The point needs to be made that it is risky not to recruit someone with the basic capability and skills. At the most basic level, this means that academic or technical qualifications should be identified and used as criteria for selection. This kind of assessment is easier in a team concerned with research or applied technology than in a general operational group.

Technical and professional skills become obsolete and people forget knowledge that is rarely used. The amount of activity arising from previous professional training can gradually deteriorate until it seems almost nonexistent.

In addition to the slow decline in the individual effectiveness of professional training, there are new concepts, methods, and applications being developed in almost all fields. Making one's technical qualifications up-to-date and relevant involves more than having a passing acquaintance with innovations. New ways of thinking should be understood in depth.

A team is more than an assembly of individual talents. It can be thought of as an organism in its own right, and the capabilities of its members should balance each other. For example, consider a gang of master criminals who intend to steal a famous diamond. The following talents are included in the gang:

- A boss — to train the team for the assignment and manage it.
- A planner — to analyze situations, propose tactics, and communicate them.
- A watchout — to provide data on the forces of law.
- A heavy (or two) — to carry equipment and deal with interruptions.
- A safe-cracker — to gain entry to the safe or vault.
- A driver — to expedite departure.

The gang may not need one person for each function because some of the criminals will be able to perform several roles. Nevertheless, the gang as a whole must have the right mix of talents, and it will be more likely to succeed if it has flexibility.

One of a team's chief advantages is a spread of talent. For one thing, it makes it possible for people to perform more frequently the activities that they enjoy. It is valuable to identify the strengths of group members and build on them within the context of the team's goals.

Although the realistic recognition of individual strengths can aid effectiveness, there appear to be national differences in expressing this recognition. In the United States, managers frequently present themselves with the professionalism of a television newscaster, while in England, it is occasionally considered impolite to ascribe the slightest virtue to oneself.

Individual members influence the climate of the group and add hard-to-define qualities such as drive, balance, judgment, openness, and strength. A team also needs an appropriately balanced mix of these personal contributions. An example might be the three-person negotiation team that contains one person with excellent judgment, another capable of clear analysis of information, and a third who has an approachable social manner.

Teams need to be balanced both technically and emotionally. Much development can occur if individuals are open to learning and change. However, the team will mature much more quickly if it has been designed with care.

SUGGESTED ACTIVITIES FOR BLOCKAGE / GENERATOR II: SUITABLE MEMBERSHIP

Activity Number & Title

11. Team Skills Audit
12. Selecting a New Team Member
13. Use Us, We're the Best

III. Team Commitment

REVIEW QUESTIONS

3. Most of the members feel that the aims of the team are hardly worthwhile.
15. Team members are not really committed to the success of the team.
27. I do not feel a strong sense of belonging to the team.
39. I am not prepared to put myself out for the team.
51. Some team members find it difficult to commit themselves to doing the job well.
63. I wish I could feel more motivated by working in this team.
75. No one is trying hard to make this a winning team.
87. If a team member gets into difficulties, he usually is left to cope with them by himself.
99. Team members are committed to individual goals at the expense of the team.

A team requires attention and time from its members. Their membership involves an element of sacrifice because each of them gives up some autonomy and self-interest. Inevitably, conflicts arise between the interests of the team and the individuals who comprise it.

The growth of commitment is a very important phase in the maturation of a team; and it often is more a matter of feeling than logic. Committed team members feel that the goals and output of the team are worthwhile and personally satisfying. They are prepared, indeed eager, to put themselves out for the team.

One test of team commitment is to question the level of the members' enjoyment of each other. A team that is close has fun, and there is a genuine concern between individuals. The members seek each other for counsel, conversation, and support; and they deepen their knowledge of each other as people. When a member leaves the team, it is a significant event and is marked in some personal way.

Committed team members value the contributions of the other members and express their good feelings openly. They try to identify positive contributions and make these explicit. This has the effect of strengthening individuals and encouraging the expression of creativity and energy.

A mature team will pour its resources into helping a team member who is having difficulties. This is an opportunity for people to show that they care, even though their collective back might be against the wall, and provide support and practical help.

Mutual support also can be disadvantageous and can lead a team to tolerate inadequate performance or protect some members from the cold drafts of corporate evaluation. In the long run, this is unhelpful because inadequate members cannot be carried without weakening team effectiveness.

TWO CONDITIONS FOR INCREASING TEAM COMMITMENT

Shared Goals

The condition of shared goals develops when a team has clarified and shared its aims and has ensured that all its members feel the goals are both achievable and important.

Processes might exist that allow individual members to gear their actions towards achievement of the goals. Members become cynical if the team's expressed goals are seen as being impossible to achieve, too wooly, or "pie in the sky." Frustration and disillusionment are the consequences of failing to ensure that action follows insight.

Personal Warmth

Personal warmth is likely to be expressed by team members in such phrases as "It's great to have you aboard" and "It feels good to work here."

Developed teams show a high degree of interpersonal respect and understanding among their members. This is built on a strong mutual understanding and tolerance of the quirks, strengths, and weaknesses of each member. Such teams also are likely to have a shared understanding of how to use the strengths and contributions of each member most effectively for the team as a whole. The members are not afraid to give and receive straight personal feedback because they are confident that it is intended to be supportive and helpful.

Commitment can be consciously developed by teams that deliberately put time aside for commitment-building activities. We think it is important that these activities become the norms of organizational behavior. In other words, they become part of "the way we do things around here."

SUGGESTED ACTIVITIES FOR BLOCKAGE/GENERATOR III:
TEAM COMMITMENT

Activity Number & Title

14. Test Your Commitment
15. Increasing Team Commitment: An Adventure Project
16. Team Counseling
17. The Commitment Problem

IV. Team Climate

REVIEW QUESTIONS

4. People in this team often are not really frank and open with each other.

16. In group discussion, team members often hide their real motives.

28. It would be helpful if the team could have "clear-the-air" sessions more often.

40. Important issues often are "swept under the carpet" and not worked through.

52. There is too much stress placed on conformity.

64. Differences between team members rarely are properly worked through.

76. Individuals in this team do not really get to know each other as people.

88. There are cliques and political maneuvering in the team.

100. Disagreements between team members are seldom worked through thoroughly and individual viewpoints are not fully heard.

As a new team begins to develop, its informal rules quickly become established and influence the group's moment-to-moment events. Although the guidelines within which the group operates rarely are written down, they are well understood. After a while, these become habitual and are transferred to new team members. The amalgam of traditions, habits, relationships, practices, rules, beliefs, and attitudes that becomes characteristic of a group is called its *climate*.

Much of the responsibility for establishing a group's climate falls on those with authority in the group. However, since that authority comes from several sources—seniority, position, expertise, and personal power—questions of authority must be sorted out in order to have a consistent definition of the behavior expected of team members.

OPEN CLIMATE

Not all group climates support the development of a team approach. Team building requires a group climate of openness—a norm of airing problems and matters of concern. A level of openness must exist for team members to establish relationships that are genuine and close.

Openness has a major impact on interpersonal relationships, and it is not an easily achieved or maintained characteristic. Too many people have learned to hide feelings and thoughts they feel are unacceptable. It is vital to team building that team members are prepared to take risks and suggest initiatives. It should be possible for them to be wrong without being made to look foolish. A chief of the NASA organization expressed the idea brilliantly when he said, "We do not punish error, we only punish the suppression of error."

Advantages and Disadvantages of Openness

The degree of openness in a team affects its climate so profoundly that it is worth identifying the advantages and disadvantages of an open approach. The advantages of a more open approach are:

- Inner frustration is avoided.
- Closer personal relationships are established.
- Problems are clarified and can be dealt with.
- Valid feedback is given, enabling others to learn and develop.
- Energy is released as issues become unblocked.
- The stultifying side effects of bureaucracy are lessened.

However, there are also potential hazards in group openness:

- The individual becomes more specific and, therefore, is more vulnerable.
- Unsureness is exposed and can be interpreted as weakness.
- Others may feel threatened by and become hostile towards an individual.
- Difficult-to-handle problems are brought into the open.

POLITICAL CLIMATE

In recent years, our knowledge of interactions between people has been extended by descriptions of psychological transactions and strategies based on ulterior motives, which transactional anlaysis refers to as "games."

Psychological games between people are part of a struggle for control and reflect the individual's need to reinforce his theory of life. As a "political" approach to team management, game-playing prevents the development of a constructive team climate.

The following negative interpersonal transactions, or games, which are briefly described in the terminology of transactional analysis, apply to both men and women "players." We emphasize that the games identified here are merely a sample; there are many more.

Kick Me . . . Some people set themselves up for psychological punishment, for instance by failing to do an expected job. The self-styled victim gets "a smart kick" and goes away to lick his wounds, feeling justified in maintaining a negative view of life.

If It Weren't For You . . . Individual failure is excused as being caused not by the person (under control) but by forces outside the person (not under control). Consequently, the player feels not responsible because he has been "unfairly" treated.

Yes, But . . . This is a superiority strategy, or "ego trip," whereby a manager appears reasonable but is, in fact, closed to suggestions. It most typically is played by managers who respond to suggestions or ideas with the phrase Yes, (implying an open and receptive mind) *but* . . . (leading into destroying the idea). A sophisticated development of this game is called "Blemish." This often is played by managers who set out to destroy a suggestion or report by picking on a minor blemish, such as grammar or punctuation, ignoring the virtues and content of the report. They destroy the work on the basis of its blemishes. It is a way of feeling good by demonstrating that others are less valuable (not OK) than oneself.

I've Got Too Much To Do . . . In this game, a manager takes on mountains of work, spends every waking hour up to his ears in papers, and finally proves to himself that he cannot cope. The payoff is feeling depressed and being unable to contribute. In a way, the person is saying, "Look, I tried my best, but I'm not able to make it." This feeling of being honestly defeated can be a comfortable position of self-justified isolation.

I Lead a Frugal Life So . . . This strategy of superiority stems from an unspoken attitude expressed by "I don't waste things nor am I extravagant, so I'm more honorable than you." This use of humbleness is a way of putting distance between the player and people and is another isolationist tactic.

There Is No Way Out, So What Can You Do? . . . After evaluating all his options, the player has decided that each choice has drawbacks. So, the logical thing to do is just sit back and let things go because "after all, there is nothing worthwhile to aim for, is there?"

Let Me Help You . . . The player collects his payoff from feeling more charitable, sensitive, and self-denying than another. Sometimes there is a vicious competition to see which player is the most self-effacing.

I've Got a Wooden Leg, So What Can You Expect of Me . . . The player uses a particular characteristic (such as color, accent, background, height) as a way of saying, "With my handicap no one can expect me to make good." Again, this is a way of feeling justified through failure.

You're Fine Except For . . . This is an odd game, in which the player uses some negative, often minor, characteristics as a way of disparaging a person. It is a technique for achieving distance and prevents valuing the contribution of the person as a whole.

Now I've Got You, You Son of a Bitch . . . By finding an excuse to make others suffer, some people satisfy a need in themselves. Dedicated players of this game often will demonstrate superhuman patience and skill in waiting for a potential victim to make a mistake (they may even mislead the victim into making the mistake) and then pounce on the victim. "After all," the person may say subconsciously, "If I can make someone suffer, then I must be important."

Although games underlie many of the interactions between people, effective teams place a value on authentic relationships and try to purge games from the currency of interactions.

The capacity to deal with interpersonal problems is a good test of team climate. A team that practices effective interpersonal problem-solving combines both confrontation and care for individual viewpoints. The skills of listening are particularly helpful. With a disagreement or communication breakdown occurs between members (e.g., John and Bob) the team should work at identifying whether:

- There is no problem between John and Bob; it is just an illusion.
- The problem is particularly felt by John.
- The problem is solely felt by Bob.
- Both John and Bob feel they have a problem.
- There is a basic difference in beliefs and values between John and Bob, therefore new information will not change matters greatly.

It often is worthwhile to clarify the different sides of an interpersonal problem by using one's own personal position as a starting-off point. The steps in this encounter may be seen from the following key questions:

- How do I want the relationship to end up?

- What specific behaviors of the other person are a problem for me?
- What effect does the other person's behavior have on me?
- What changes in behavior would I like to see?
- Can I clearly state the problem and tell how I feel without confusing or blaming the other person?
- If the other person becomes defensive or aggressive, do I practice listening skills?
- How effectively can I use systematic problem-solving approaches to deal with difficult decisions?
- Do we both negotiate "space" for ourselves, so that conflicts of values have minimum impact?

There are three interconnecting features of a constructive team climate. These exist when the members have skills in interpersonal relationships, respect and warmth between themselves, and are supported in their openness by those with power and influence.

SUGGESTED ACTIVITIES FOR BLOCKAGE/GENERATOR IV: TEAM CLIMATE

Activity Number & Title

18. Team-Climate Questionnaire
19. From Me to You, From You to Me
20. Cave Rescue

V. Team Achievement

REVIEW QUESTIONS

5. The objectives of our team are not really clear.
17. In practice, the team rarely achieves its objectives.
29. In practice, low levels of achievement are accepted.
41. Individuals are given few incentives to stretch themselves.
53. Energy is absorbed in unproductive ways and does not go into getting results.
65. No time is devoted to questioning whether our efforts have been worthwhile.
77. We seem more concerned about giving a good appearance than achieving results.
89. Nothing that we do could be described as excellent.
101. We often fail to finish things satisfactorily.

Teams exist to achieve results; this is their primary purpose. It makes sense to evaluate teams on their ability to "deliver the goods." When a team meets its members' needs for social contact, but fails to perform, it is failing the critical test of achieving tangible results.

Effective team achievement requires clear objectives that are shared by the members. These objectives affect the vitality of a group because they focus energy and supply a means of measurement. However, generating clear and shared objectives requires more skill than usually is realized. Teams that function within an organization also find that they need to clarify and validate their objectives with other teams and functions in that organization.

It is one thing to set objectives and quite another to put them into practice. When a team fails to meet its objectives, it needs to explore the process and resolve the sense of failure before that feeling has a corrosive effect on morale. The techniques of critiquing can help turn "failure" into a development opportunity for the team.

Since almost all developments experience troughs or setbacks at some point, a team should be able to handle both practical setbacks and the emotional side-effects of temporary failure. Here, resilience and innovation are appropriate team tactics to continue achievement despite difficulties.

An effective team sets high standards of achievement, which, in turn, are influential in determining how the team operates. Although achieving a high standard of performance is a satisfying personal accomplishment, the standards are maintained through group pressure. Accordingly, it is important to work as a team on defining standards, or norms, so that performance levels are set above the acceptable level and the team strives towards excellence.

Achievement should be valued and rewarded within the team. The rewards do not have to be financial, although it is deluding to consider material rewards as irrelevant. One reward for people who achieve highly is their sense of personal significance and potency. An increased involvement in decision making and communication are rewards in themselves. Additionally, they stretch themselves and learn new skills that bring a sense of movement and vitality.

Some teams become very concerned with their image, particularly if their function cannot clearly justify itself through concrete output. They give excessive and indulgent attention to good public relations rather than to tangible achievement. In its worst form, this concern leads to empire building and the distribution of organizational resources on the basis of charisma rather than effectiveness.

Highly effective teams review how they use their resources with consideration for their "return on investment." Their question is "How far is our work actually producing results?" Much can be learned from the behavior of a team of NASA engineers who discovered that the lunar-landing module they had constructed was too heavy. They rigorously examined each component and made a piece by piece evaluation, reviewing the benefit of each unit and simplifying at every stage. They pared down each unit to its simplest and lightest form. This kind of vigorous review of benefit against criteria is directly applicable to team achievement and offers a powerful basis for increasing a team's effectiveness.

SUGGESTED ACTIVITIES FOR BLOCKAGE / GENERATOR V:
TEAM ACHIEVEMENT

Activity Number & Title

21. Defining the Team's Maintenance and Achievement Activities
22. Identifying Team Success
23. New Game

VI. Relevant Corporate Role

REVIEW QUESTIONS

6. Team members are unsure about the team's contribution to the wider organization.

18. Our team's contribution is not clearly understood by other parts of the organization.

30. If the team were disbanded, the organization would not feel the loss.

42. There is confusion between the work of this team and the work of others.

54. The role of our team is not clearly identified within the organization.

66. We do not have an adequate way to establish our team's objectives and strategy.

78. The organization does not use the vision and skills that the team has to offer.

90. The team's objectives have not been systematically related to the objectives of the whole organization.

102. We do not work within clear strategic guidelines.

One link between the team manager and the wider organization is illustrated by an experience of a company that has an annual event known as "budget cutting." At budget-cutting time, department managers submitted their budgets and then waited for the 20 to 30 percent surgery that usually came. In anticipation of the event, the managers inflated their estimates to ensure that they would have sufficient budget provision after the cuts were made.

Then came the year that the senior manager group decided to change the policy and accept budget estimates without surgery. The result was chaotic. The managers had to spend their unexpected surplus funds and then justify the expenditure. As a consequence, the managers expected the same response in the following year, and they presented budget proposals with no fat at all. However, the senior manager group reverted to their previous style and slashed 25 percent off all estimates. More chaos resulted.

This case illustrates how the lack of consistent policy and objectives left team managers with little choice but to protect their groups and develop defensive and negative stances against their organization. If a team's contribution is going to be worthwhile, it must be relevant to the objectives of the wider organization, and those objectives must be understood. Since the mechanisms for building broad corporate objectives are often rusty and inefficient, senior teams should spend time in reviewing how they establish and communicate objectives.

Team effectiveness involves clarifying and negotiating a useful role in relation to the wider organization. This requires skills and processes which, by definition, cross the boundaries between teams. The importance of this interchange is hard to underestimate. Teams that are insular and convoluted undermine organizational effectiveness.

It is inevitable that the wider organization will exercise some control over its constituent parts. However, the manner and extent of organization control is never a clear issue. It is a topic on which senior managers often feel disposed to philosophize.

When excessive direction alienates individuals from their sense of potency, their work becomes humdrum and mechanical. Resistance movements spread and "ain't it awful about them" becomes a constant theme of conversation. On the other hand, insufficient direction can provoke a wasteland of indecision or energetic irrelevance. This fragmentation of direction allows endless duplication and oversights.

Teams need to know fully their contribution to the wider organization, and the organization needs to know and value what each team contributes. The relevant questions here are:

- How can the team fit into the organization as a whole?

- What contribution does the team make to the organizational system?

- Are there sufficient mechanisms for clarifying the optimum roles for the team?

The issues here are more abstract than the more tangible issues of internal team effectiveness. It is like comparing a householder cultivating his own back yard with the town planner who is responsible for the community environment. The quality of the immediate environment depends on how each householder minds his own plot of land, but, when taken together, the individual decisions made by householders profoundly affect the wider environment. It is this relationship that has to be explored and developed. One householder may dream of building a skyscraper on his plot, but this is likely to be out of keeping with the surrounding community.

An organization operates as a system comprised of interlocking and individual parts. Its effectiveness depends on how each part interacts with the others to produce whatever goods and services are being created. Some groups are more closely involved than others with the constructive processes of the organization.

In a manufacturing organization, the production department is clearly in the middle of the core process. The core process is the central activity (or activities) that generates the key outputs of the organization. In a manufacturing organization, it is the process that produces the products. In a service organization, core processes generate the services purchased by the customer.

Other groups are involved in supporting the core-process groups in one way or another. It is important for team members to have a clear understanding of the core processes of the organization and their role in the achievement of primary outputs.

When there is overlap in the roles assigned to teams in an organization, problems can arise; often activities can be duplicated by different teams without the sharing of information between them. Difficulties also occur when there is too much difference in departmental practices, such as that between research and development departments ("We want the best technical solution, engineered to the highest standards.") and manufacturing departments ("We need the simplest product using the cheapest materials."). Steps need to be taken to ensure that systems of values and judgments developed by teams are within the broad limits established for the organization as a whole.

A dilemma faced by large organizations that have a head office or group function and various outlying businesses is shown by questions such as: Who do we serve?; Are we supposed to lead?; To control?; To provide a service?; To intervene by right?; To intervene by request?

These are difficult questions, but they can be clarified through the idea of a core process. Since this can only be properly defined towards the top of the organization, it is a particular responsibility of senior groups to spend time acquiring the skills of analysis, conducting reviews, and engaging with subordinate teams to ensure that organizational and team goals harmonize as much as possible.

SUGGESTED ACTIVITIES FOR BLOCKAGE / GENERATOR VI:
CORPORATE ROLE

Activity Number & Title

24. Organizational Role
25. Mapping the Organization
26. Team Survival

VII. Effective Work Methods

REVIEW QUESTIONS

7. We rarely achieve much progress in team meetings.

19. When the team is having a meeting, we do not listen to each other.

31. The team meetings often seem to lack a methodical approach.

43. Team members rarely plan or prepare for meetings.

55. The team does not set aside time to consider and review how it tackles problems.

67. We often seem to get bogged down when a difficult problem is being discussed in team meetings.

79. We have team meetings, but do not properly examine their purpose.

91. Decisions made at meetings are not properly recorded or activated.

103. Our meetings do not properly resolve all the issues that should be dealt with.

Committees and groups are notorious for confused debate, boring repetition, and poor decision making. Much time and opportunity is wasted during ineffectual meetings and they often conclude with everyone present feeling dispirited, confused, and frustrated.

However, people need to learn how to use meetings successfully and creatively in order to develop clarity, commitment, and high energy for action. Since those attending a meeting should be clear about the purpose and goals of the session, a helpful question to ask is "What do we wish to achieve in this meeting?" The goals then can be clarified and serve to focus activity.

DECISION-MAKING STYLES

There are several identifiable styles of decision making in teams, which can be described as categories on a continuum, similar to that shown in Figure 5.

One person decides.	A small group (the "in" people) decide.	The decision is taken by a majority.	The team discusses the problem and comes to a consensus.	The team comes to a unanimous conclusion.

Figure 5. A decision-making continuum.

As the team goes towards the right-hand end of the decision-making continuum, the degree of personal commitment shown by team members increases markedly. However, a more developed team is required to handle the added complexity of these team styles.

It is helpful for all team members to know the "name of the game" in relation to decision making. Prior to working through a problem, the team can explicitly determine which approach to adopt. Here the team manager's style is the key because moving to the right of the decision-making continuum involves sharing influence with the team.

LISTENING SKILLS

Effective team meetings require team members with developed skills in listening. Although listening often is considered a passive condition, it is exactly the opposite. In fact, listening is hard work and requires definite commitment and personal discipline. The listener must deliberately prepare to listen and the quality of that listening deteriorates as he is carried away with the events of the moment.

Perhaps the chief requirement for effective listening is to "have room" to attend to others. If you are preoccupied with your own thoughts and feelings, you will not be available to actively listen. People who give relaxed, open attention to others are rated as effective listeners and better recall what has been said. Active listeners signal their attention and availability both verbally ("I would like to listen to you now") and nonverbally (by not fidgeting or looking bored, etc.).

When listening, it is helpful to try to understand the other person's view without superimposing your own views or judgments prematurely. One sure way to prevent communication is to jump in with your own viewpoint before the other person has been able to fully express his point. Such discussions frequently deteriorate into wrangles.

Active listening shows others that you respect and value their contribution. It may be difficult to accept the idea that the differences between people offer a resource for progress; but if you can manage to bridge differences, there is much of value to be gained. The following are some useful techniques that can help listening:

Checking: "Can I repeat what you said in order to check my own understanding?"

Clarifying: "It seems to me that this is what you mean . . . "

Showing Support: "I hear you. Please carry on."

Building on: "Building on your last point, I would add . . . "

Structuring: "Shall we look at the symptoms, try to define the problem, and then discuss possible solutions?"

Teams that have a low level of listening show the following characteristics:

- Dominance by a few members;
- Crosstalk (several members talking at once);
- Ideas lost (no mechanism for catching and retaining points);
- Repetitive contributions;
- Wordy inputs (individuals use much speaking time for little content);
- Turned-off members;
- Inability to handle consensus decision making.

A team that sets a high standard of listening usually is enjoyed by its members. The group is generally effective and individuals feel a high commitment to the other members.

PROBLEM-SOLVING CYCLE

The quality of a team's output is greatly affected by its skills as a problem-solving unit. Although disciplines are indispensable, there is no problem-solving formula that teams can use successfully without adaptation. It seems that modifying "off the shelf" methods to suit the personalities and context of a group is necessary, and in the process, the team develops by identifying its own unique approach. One starting point is to test a sequential program, such as the following six-step approach.

Step One: Objectives

The aim of this first step is to arrive at a shared understanding of the task by identifying both the *broad* objectives—why the task is being undertaken— and also the *specific* objectives—the concrete goals to be achieved.

Step Two: Success Criteria

One of the most useful topics that a group can discuss is "When do we know that we have successfully completed the task?" This question makes it possible for everyone to have a clear idea of the required end performance. Hence, just enough energy can be expended to accomplish the task adequately with the best possible use of time.

Step Three: Information

Group members possess facts, opinions, feelings, and ideas about their situation and the problem in hand. Sometimes, external data also are available. It often is useful to be aware of the data that are missing. In many ways the quality of a final outcome is a function of the ability of the group to ferret out relevant information and organize all the data in a comprehensible way.

Step Four: Plans

Military pundits make a useful distinction between strategy and tactics. The strategy level looks at broad definitions of What Has To Be Done (WHTBD) and the tactics level deals with specific WHTBDs. Action groups should have both a clear visualization of the broad plan and of the specific, often individual, steps to be taken.

Step Five: Action

The task is initiated and completed as specified in the plans. If this cycle is followed, the action taken will be relevant to the team's objectives and criteria will have been developed that indicate when the action has been successful. Above all, if the previous steps in the cycle have been thoroughly completed, there will be sufficient understanding of the reasoning behind the actions to allow for flexibility and amendment during the action phase.

Step Six: Review To Improve

People learn from seeing the results of action. This feedback information should be collected, clarified, considered, and shaped into new ground rules. Without feedback there is little chance to change and develop; people simply repeat the same patterns. The adage "practice makes perfect" is idealistic; a more accurate observation is "practice makes permanent." Bad practices can be made as permanent as good ones. When groups review the processes of their work together, they gain the information necessary for rapidly developing a strong and effective team.

To remain effective, teams must continuously review the whole cycle of systematic problem solving to winnow out ineffective practices and build on existing strengths. When time is allocated to this review, there are many opportunities for the group to develop and learn from experience. Reviewing for improvement is introduced by asking "What lessons can we learn from this experience to help us in the future?"

The problem-solving cycle serves a useful purpose if it is checked out and adapted to meet a team's particular needs. It is not necessary to adhere to the pattern if it seems inappropriate. Often one task will require recycling several times to achieve the required result, or individual steps can be extended considerably.

TEAM EFFECTIVENESS

A team needs the following conditions in order to succeed:

- *Task Effectiveness:* The abilities and methods to complete a task effectively.
- *Good Group Climate:* An atmosphere or climate that encourages and values the contributions of team members.
- *No (or a Low Amount of) Destructive Behaviors:* The actions or behaviors that delay the group, take it away from its objectives, and cause problems between its members.

Checklist

The following checklist[1] can help you to evaluate the effectiveness of your team.

TASK EFFECTIVENESS

1. Does the group use a *methodical approach?*
2. Are *resources* (things and people) used effectively?

---

[1]This checklist draws on some ideas presented in "Role Functions in a Group," in J. William Pfeiffer and John E. Jones (Eds.), *The 1976 Annual Handbook for Group Facilitators.* La Jolla, CA: University Associates, 1976, 136-138.

3. Are ideas and activities *coordinated* (by a person or plan)?
4. Do members *seek and give information* and opinions?
5. Are *ideas expanded* and tested in the group?
6. Do *summarizing* and restating of ideas and suggestions occur?
7. Is *action initiated* and do members act with energy?

GROUP CLIMATE

1. Are members *encouraged and supported?*
2. Are members' *contributions valued* and accepted?
3. Are *members* brought into discussions and given a chance to be *heard*?
4. Does the group *set standards* for itself to use in choosing procedures and evaluating decisions?
5. Is the *feeling* in the group *expressed* and are personal issues dealt with?
6. Do members thoughtfully (rather than begrudgingly) *accept the decisions* of the group?

DESTRUCTIVE BEHAVIOR

1. Do members *withdraw* from the group by daydreaming, whispering to others, or wandering from the subject?
2. Is *competition* with others in the group expressed by attempts to offer the most ideas, play the most roles, talk most?
3. Are members *aggressive,* criticizing or blaming others and showing hostility or deflating others?
4. Do members use the group for *self-confession,* excessively delving into personal, nongroup-oriented feelings or points of view?
5. Do members *disrupt the work* of the group by clowning and horsing around or being flippant?
6. Is there *special pleading,* introducing suggestions related to members' own concerns, and lobbying?
7. Do members *block* the progress of the group by going off on a tangent, arguing too much on a point, and rejecting ideas without consideration?

Skills of an Effective Team

Certain team skills, taken together, complete a useful definition of effective process. The key skills are:

- Clear identification of objectives;
- Establishing criteria to measure effectiveness;
- Information-analysis techniques;
- Generating options for action;
- Comprehensive planning;
- Energetic action;
- Careful and open review of performance;
- Appropriate control;
- Active listening.

An effective team will have honed its working methods so that they become an informal discipline. The team quickly gets moving and maintains a rapid pace, but its high level of personal attention and economy of expression means that relevant issues are explored. Individual members have developed personal skills that are appreciated and utilized by the team. There is an air of competence, and boredom is rarely felt at meetings.

SUGGESTED ACTIVITIES FOR BLOCKAGE / GENERATOR VII: EFFECTIVE WORK METHODS

Activity Number & Title

27. How Good Are Your Meetings?
28. Why/How Charting
29. Effective Problem-Solving Survey

VIII. Team Organization

REVIEW QUESTIONS

8. The objectives of some individual team members do not gel with those of other members.

20. Team members are uncertain about their individual roles in relation to the team.

32. There is no regular review of individual objectives and priorities.

44. If team members are missing, their work just does not get done.

56. Much improvement is needed in communication between team members.

68. The team does not have adequate administrative resources and procedures.

80. We function in rather a rigid manner and are not sufficiently flexible in using team resources.

92. Team members could collaborate much more if they examined the possibilities of doing so on a person-by-person basis.

104. We do not examine how the team spends its time and energy.

A team is comprised of people who probably have several different roles to perform and affect others in the way they interrelate. One person may choose to play his role in a particular manner that affects others profoundly. We have known teams in which the "success" of one member would automatically result in the "failure" of another. Problems also arise when individuals are unsure of their roles and how they relate to the output of the team.

When team roles are unclear or conflicting, mechanisms are required to clarify them and work through role conflicts. The solution is to work through what is expected of each team member in his work and then to check it out with the whole team to clarify any confusion and possible overlap. Again, teams usually live in dynamic environments, and this can result in changes in work requirements. It pays to have regular reviews of the team's goals and individuals' objectives.

Although clear role definition is an important prerequisite to individual achievement, it is important not to carry this to the point of rigidity. One strength of a team is that it thrives on mutual support and interdependence. "It's not my job" is a negative and damaging response to a team colleague who is in need of support. Team members may have a primary role in the life of the team, but they also should identify what parts of their jobs may be in support of others.

A planned program develops the strength and resourcefulness of a team by defining primary roles, supporting roles, and the ways in which team members can learn by working with others. In some organizations, programs of "job swapping" within teams are used to increase interdependence, reduce possible obsolescence of people, and develop team and organizational resources.

Last, but not least, teams usually have a "sharp-end" function—achieving the team's mission—and supporting functions. Energy and resources may be poured into a team's sharp-end activities without thought to the essential support and administration that is required. This is like having an army that moves without supply lines and gets three-quarters of the way to its destination, then discovers there is no fuel and food left. A team needs to balance the change towards achievement with support and administrative organization.

LARGE TEAMS

As a rule of thumb, we define a large team as one that has more than ten members. Large teams present special problems of coordination to management. The following checklist highlights typical problems and offers some suggestions for resolving them.

1. Poor Leadership

One problem faced by large groups is the choice of a leader. Since large groups are difficult to organize, they often require a more disciplined approach. The leader needs skills in structuring a large group's work and keeping the energy level high. Frequently, the leader is responsible for clarifying the group's objectives and gaining the members' commitment to them.

2. Flagging Interest

In a large group, it is difficult for individuals to contribute fully because there simply is not enough time for people to have their say. As a consequence, members may become frustrated and withdrawn; they may lose their identification with the group's task and their commitment to its achievement. Since personal contacts are more remote in a large group, the bonds of closeness are less developed.

3. Excessive Information

The larger the group, the more information is available, both in the form of data and as individual and discrepant perceptions. This makes it difficult for the members to structure information clearly and then make good quality decisions from that base.

4. Confusion of Organizational Role

Groups often are uncertain about their roles within an organization. Without understanding their group's value to the organization, individual members may follow their own primary job objectives, rather than committing their time and energy to the large groups.

5. Hidden Personal Conflicts

In large groups, it is easy for personal differences to be hidden while they continue to fester. When personal conflicts occur, it is important to work them through, but large groups rarely have a framework for doing this. Therefore, the group members are likely to be much more concerned with "politics."

6. Insufficient Structure

Large groups require imaginative use of techniques to structure their time and resources. This involves both the mastery of those techniques and being able to divide the group into subgroups in a flexible way.

7. Low Personal Skills

Individual skills, such as listening, building on ideas, and clear presentation, often are practiced less in large groups. As a consequence, when individuals become frustrated, they may lose their personal discipline and the quality of individual attention in the group deteriorates. When individuals are unclear about their contribution to a group and remain unable to define a useful role for themselves, the group experiences difficulty in structuring itself.

8. Unclear Decision Making

Without a formal organization, groups often find it difficult to identify the decision-making procedure, which should include all members, be explicit, and be maintained in practice. Consensus decision making can be very difficult in large groups. Therefore, without high quality personal skills, it may be necessary to use other forms of decision making to get things done. One useful idea is to set a time limit and make the best decision possible within that scale.

Both large and small teams should examine their day-to-day organization to ensure that communication, roles, objectives, and procedures enable results to be achieved and morale to be high. This theme is never fully exhausted. A team is never fully organized; it is always in the process of organizing.

SUGGESTED ACTIVITES FOR BLOCKAGE / GENERATOR VIII:
TEAM ORGANIZATION

Activity Number & Title

30. Team Mission and Individual Objectives
31. Team Communication
32. Start Up
33. How Do We Make Decisions?

IX. Critiquing

REVIEW QUESTIONS

9. When team members are criticized, they often feel that they have lost face.

21. Members often restrain their critical remarks to avoid "rocking the boat."

33. The team is not good at learning from its mistakes.

45. Attempts to review events critically are seen as negative and harmful.

57. We would benefit from an impartial assessment of how we work.

69. We lack the skills to review our effectiveness constructively.

81. Performance would improve if constructive criticism were encouraged.

93. Little time is spent on reviewing what the team does, how it works, and how to improve it.

105. We make resolutions but, basically, we don't learn from our mistakes.

Some teams operate an informal conspiracy; they refuse to review events in an analytical and critical way. Such teams inhibit the free flow of judgment and comment. Withholding criticism can be done for several reasons:

- *Politeness.* Team members may feel that social etiquette precludes confrontation.

- *Fear of "Loss of Face."* Individuals may see criticism as an unwelcome whittling down of their self-image.

- *Disinclination To "Rock the Boat."* Team members may see criticism as exposing weaknesses and undermining morale.

- *Inadequate Skills.* Team members appreciate the benefits of intensive review but simply do not feel able to handle this constructively. They lack the required skills of analysis and personal confrontation.

Reviewing both specific projects and routine working provides valuable learning for the team. We call this aspect of team work *critique.* This means that individuals gather to analyze the strengths and weaknesses of their performance, are open about their personal assessments, and can take negative comments without rancor.

Critique helps the team to evolve. There is no short cut through development; it requires that people question the status quo. Although both positive and negative observations are valuable, in practice, it is not easy to use either positive or negative feedback. Positive comment can lead group members to unwarranted preening and complacency, and negative inputs may be interpreted as sabotage and provoke a dispute.

Open critique can be especially threatening to senior team members. As the architects of the existing order they feel a greater sense of ownership. Hence, their self-esteem can be more at risk. Our friend, psychologist Barry A. Goodfield, supports critique with this statement, "There is a choice. You can advance to growth, or retreat to security." Individuals who can use feedback constructively have acquired a valuable asset. They can grow from error or inadequacy.

Initially, critique sessions are best conducted away from the busy fragmentation of work. Later, critique skills can be readily integrated within team meetings and, informally, between team members. The following guidelines may be used for your critiquing sessions.

AVOID	TRY TO
Talking too much.	State your points simply and one at a time.
Jumping in and quickly moving on.	Explore ideas and feelings in depth, and find concrete examples of your points.
Glossing over problems.	Explore difficulties and their causes thoroughly, using a "What can we do about them" approach.

AVOID	TRY TO
Raising false hopes.	Set a "contract" between yourselves that you believe is realistic.
Taking a parental tone.	Stay in the "adult" or rational part of yourselves, because the "parent" part of us tends to respond with condescending judgment.
Not taking the process seriously.	Make it evident that you value the process enough to spend time seriously discussing these issues.
Being inconsistent.	Ask whether you appear inconsistent and clarify all apparent inconsistencies.
Criticizing a person's ambitions or evaluations (the "putdown").	Find out why the person has this view; contribute information and options rather than judgment.
Making commitments too readily.	State the truth, only make a commitment if you are sure it can be honored, and set a time scale that you know is realistic.
Displaying a negative and disinterested attitude.	Give your support and energy to make a session valuable and try to use the discussion as an important opportunity to improve.
Solving others' problems.	Encourage others to suggest their own solutions and not depend too much on you.
Using targets as potential weapons.	Set targets for learning rather than for discipline.
Seeing only one way ahead.	Be flexible and look carefully at options, even if you decide to discard them later.

The skillful practice of methodical critique consistently develops standards. As team members learn to express their judgments, they gain strength and release energy that was blocked through inhibited expression. The concept of responsibility is extended and becomes more willingly sought. As a whole, the team benefits.

SUGGESTED ACTIVITIES FOR BLOCKAGE / GENERATOR IX: CRITIQUING

Activity Number & Title

  1. Giving Feedback
34. Like and Don't Like
35. The Best and the Worst
36. You Should Have Been a . . .

X. Individual Development

REVIEW QUESTIONS

10. New team members often are just left to find their own place in the team.

22. The potential of some team members is not being developed.

34. Team members tend not to show initiative in keeping up-to-date or in developing themselves.

46. Little time and effort is spent on individual development and training.

58. Most team members have been trained only in their technical discipline.

70. The team does not take steps to develop its members.

82. Individuals who are retiring or uncertain often are overridden.

94. A person who questions the established practices in the group probably will be smartly put back in place.

106. Individuals are not encouraged to go outside the team to widen their personal knowledge and skills.

A team is effective through its capacity to harness and coordinate the strengths of individuals. It follows that, other things being equal, the most capable teams are those with the highest level of individual talent and ability.

When new members join a team, it is important that they are introduced with understanding but firmness. An individual should not feel that he can coast gently through. The team has to make demands and membership can be considered a privilege. The team is a vehicle for expression of the individual, offering opportunities for each member to develop technically, managerially, and personally.

STRONGLY DEVELOPED INDIVIDUALS

Teams often are plagued by a member who is a loud and staunch advocate of his own viewpoint. While an outside observer may describe such a person as "strong," team members privately may describe him as "a pain." It is, therefore, important to clarify that what we mean by strength is much more than dominance. A strongly developed individual is a person who:

- Has energy;
- Is in touch with his feelings;
- Is prepared to be open about his position;
- Will change a viewpoint through reason, not subservience;
- Is prepared to take risks.

When strongly developed individuals gather together, some people are threatened. Conformity through abdication is unlikely to rule the day, and decisions are less likely to be rubber-stamped. Since abrasion and resolute assertiveness need to be tolerated and even may be enjoyed in this kind of group, the climate is less benign for the team manager, whose own skills receive greater challenge. Some individuals may feel outshone and weakened, and sometimes they withdraw into making minimal but safe contributions.

Inevitably, people vary in their capacity and possible contribution, but rarely is their potential fully realized. Achieving a greater use of that latent potential is valuable and deeply satisfying. When a person feels there are new challenges and experiences ahead, energy is released and creative ideas are generated and implemented. The individual becomes capable of handling a greater level of responsibility without losing the essential sense of inner competence. All in all, the developed person is more resourceful.

Individual development is difficult to describe because the processes are personal and the outcomes are hard to measure. The developing person has a capacity to remain open, enquiring, and experimenting. With age, discrimination grows and novelty diminishes; and, concurrently, the capacity to seriously employ new insights can also grow. The character of development changes over time, but the intensity remains. After probing what he values and believes in, the developed individual may not see himself as a neatly symmetrical and ideal person, but, instead, accepts and allows expression of all that is genuinely there.

Throughout this book we emphasize the importance of a group working through the problems and forces influencing its situations. The same is true for individuals. Personal development involves looking at the characteristic ebb and flow of energy within yourself. We value strengthening behaviors that are positive, achieving, and humanistic, at the expense of the negative and static.

PASSIVE OR ACTIVE APPROACHES

One group of experienced managers worked at trying to define different personal approaches to management, and they decided that the key distinguishing feature was how a person uses his energy. They felt that some people are predominately *passive*, while others express creativity and energy and are *active*. The somewhat controversial list that emerged through the managers' discussion includes the following characteristics:

The Passive Person

- Seeks to be undisturbed;
- Avoids self-knowledge;
- Is satisfied with trivia;
- Is programed toward failure;
- Is not in touch with his feelings;
- Lacks concern for others;
- Tries to manipulate others;
- Is over-tense physically;
- Lacks energy and vitality;
- Is generally dissatisfied with others;
- Is unhappy with life;
- Is bound by childhood habits;
- Accepts low standards;
- Gives up and avoids frustration;
- Finds he cannot give attention.

The Active Person

- Seeks challenge;
- Develops insight into himself;
- Uses time and energy as valuable resources;
- Achieves results;
- Knows and uses his feelings creatively;
- Cares for others;
- Is open and basically honest;

- Is not physically over-tense;
- Usually has a high energy level;
- Generally likes others;
- Enjoys life;
- Is relatively free of childhood hang-ups;
- Sets high standards;
- Is committed to see things through;
- Can devote good attention to situations.

Few people exhibit either an extremely active or passive approach to life. Most individuals fall somewhere in the middle of the scale, and development is a question of moving away from the passive towards the active. Active people tend to find life an adventure, enjoy variety, and always seem to end up enriched. On the other hand, passive people seem always to be in a state of inadequate adjustment to the unsatisfactory nature of things.

ASSERTIVENESS

Recently there has been a great interest in developing skills known as assertive techniques. These have important applications for team effectiveness through individual capacity. When people know what they feel and what they want, take definite and clear action to present their views, and make sure they are heard fully, then we describe them as being *assertive*. Assertive individuals can benefit both themselves and their teams.

Teams gain the following advantages from assertion:

- *Improved Decision Making:* half-baked ideas are critically screened.
- *More Initiatives:* people push ideas to improve their areas.
- *Better Use of Resources:* the loudest voice does not carry the day.
- *Real Management Development:* more active, strong, and promotable talent.

Individuals also gain advantages because assertion:

- *Gives You Energy:* helps you feel stronger.
- *Really Works:* you get important things done.
- *Improves Your Relationships:* important issues are opened.
- *Becomes Therapeutic:* you constructively express tensions.

Although these advantages sound good, there are snags. Assertive people state their positions, and that makes it easier for them to be chopped down when they are exposed. Some people may see the assertive person as a nuisance (or, at worst, as an obstinate troublemaker) and take action accordingly. If the assertive person is wrong, he can push others "up the creek without a paddle." No one applauds the architect of disaster.

It is not necessary to use assertion in every situation. Rather, it is good to acquire the skills that enable self-assertiveness and, like other management skills, use them when necessary.

Blocks To Being Assertive

Although their reason tells them that it is logical and appropriate to be assertive, some people find it very difficult. There are five difficulties that block many people, and one or two of them are likely to be important to you:

1. *Upbringing:* Those inner voices of authority that tell you "not to speak against your betters."

2. *Your Rights:* Each person has the right to be heard and taken seriously, but do you feel that this is true for you?

3. *Lack of Clarity:* Not knowing what you want in yourself and being unable to express yourself strongly and clearly.

4. *Being Afraid:* Trying to avoid disapproval or punishment from others.

5. *Being Put Off:* Allowing another's reaction or circumstances to weaken or cut off your effort.

If you have experienced an inability to assert yourself in particular situations, is there a pattern to the situations? There usually is. Maybe your difficulty is that you feel that things cannot be changed. One helpful idea is that assertion is partly a matter of attitude and partly skill. Skills can be learned and success in practicing them should lead to your feeling stronger.

Techniques for Effective Assertion

Much can be learned from watching others; even people you do not like can be a source of insight. Observe how some people seem to get their message across much more effectively than others. Try to understand the differences between people who succeed and those who do not, then you will be able to add to the following list of characteristics:

Avoid Emotional Presentation: Being angry or hurt can take your energy away from efforts toward your goal and confuse the issue. Stick to a clear, straightforward message.

Deal with One Issue at a Time: Be clear about the point you want to make and continue to work on it until you resolve the matter. Only retreat when you have made a rational decision that progress is impossible.

Be Clear and Direct: Lay the issue on the table simply and baldly. Complexity and pussy-footing are enemies of resolution.

Convey Your Feelings: Let the other person know how strongly you feel about the matter. Be honest and avoid exaggeration or false humility.

Watch Out for Flack: Other people will try to sidetrack and divert you. They may feel under pressure, so let them say their piece and return to your point.

Don't Steamroller: Since others will have a viewpoint, accept the truth in what they have to say. Tell them that you accept their point, but return to your own message.

Openly Admit Error: If you are wrong, then say this openly and directly. Sometimes people will try to make you feel weak if you make a mistake, but keep strong and try to learn from the error.

Go for the Workable Compromise: While you are working towards something you want, watch for the other person's needs and try to meet those as well as your own. That way you both win.

Assertive people are stronger resources for a team, and they feel better about themselves and their jobs. However, like all strengths, assertiveness can be abused, and strongly developed individuals can place special strains on the team manager and the team as a whole.

A mature team will take care to develop the individual competence and strength of each member. People feel the excitement that results from personal development, and this energy feeds the team as a whole. The team becomes a vehicle for each member to express his creativity. This includes developing a breadth of technical skills, increasing personal effectiveness through assertion, and, basically, having a more active, energetic, and responsible attitude toward work and relationships.

SUGGESTED ACTIVITES FOR BLOCKAGE / GENERATOR X:
INDIVIDUAL DEVELOPMENT

Activity Number & Title

37. Is It OK To Be More Me?
38. Managing People Skills Inventory
39. Good Coaching Practice

XI. Creative Capacity

REVIEW QUESTIONS

11. Not many new ideas are generated by the team.
23. Team members are wary about suggesting new ideas.
35. We have the reputation of being stick-in-the-muds.
47. This team seldom innovates anything.
59. Good ideas seem to get lost.
71. New ideas from outside the team seldom are accepted.
83. It would be fair to say the team has little vision.
95. Only a few members suggest new ideas.
107. Creative ideas often are not followed through to definite action.

It is said that Einstein, as a young man, developed the concept of the curvature of space while daydreaming about riding on a sunbeam. During wartime, a British scientist conceived of a bomb that would skip like a stone along the surface of the water before exploding against the restraining walls of German dams. Such brilliant innovations are the work of creative individuals who have progressed beyond their colleagues.

Individual brilliance is too rare a quality to be relied on entirely. Consequently, much innovation comes from teams who have specific assignments to manage creativity. Examples of this team approach range from a film production crew to vehicle design engineers. It is widely accepted that effective teams are able to generate creative ideas and put them into practice.

The process of creation is hard to describe in rational and objective terms. People often are unable to explain how an outstanding leap of imagination came to them; for example, innovators are likely to report, "It came to me in a dream" or "Everything suddenly clicked together."

A British researcher, Edward Matchett, who has studied the creative process intensively, reports that people can learn to develop their creative potential by "tuning in" to latent aspects of themselves. His research shows that creativity is aided when the person is emotionally, physically, and intellectually open.[2]

However, harnessing the brain's creativity requires more of an individual than just being open to innovation. Creativity does not have to be unplanned or haphazard. Individuals and teams can enhance their creativity by relatively straightforward techniques. We see the creative process as beginning with the identification of a need and the perception of the "missing links." Then a new idea is needed. This can be a logical extension of an existing stream of thought or a radical departure. Seldom is a new idea clear or fully worked out at its inception; it has to be developed, enlarged, extended, and simplified. If it is not to remain merely an issue for academic debate, a new idea must be tested.

The creative process can be briefly outlined in four steps, as follows:

1. Identifying the missing link.
2. Generating germs of ideas.
3. Developing mature proposals.
4. Testing proposals and absorbing the new idea.

Risk cannot be eliminated from creativity, and the most highly trained and experienced people continue to make errors. Accordingly, hand in hand with creativity must go a mature capacity to make decisions.

BLOCKAGES TO CREATIVITY

When exploring the development of high creativity capacity, it is useful to begin with what prevents people from being more creative. Common blockages to creativity can be summarized under the following five headings.

Block 1. Rigid Attitudes

Most people have a picture of how the world operates, and they persistently interpret experiences in light of that subjective framework. Of course, it is easier to see this rigidity in others than in ourselves.

---

[2]Edward Matchett & Sir George Trevelyan, *Twelve Seats at the Round Table.* Jersey, United Kingdom: Neville Speerman, 1976.

The premature defining and judging of ideas and events tends to rule out the questioning of long-established habits of thinking. Characteristically, rigid attitudes harden with experience because they are self-fulfilling. Individuals influence their experiences by their own efforts, that is, their experience justifies an attitude, which then provokes new experiences, which further demonstrate that the attitude is right.

Block 2. Poor Presentation

People who are trying to express new ideas often are unclear, repetitive, inconsistent, and difficult to comprehend. Since creativity involves moving into an unclear and unevaluated territory, the excitement of the experience can act as a barrier to effective presentation. Another barrier is the tendency to meet one's own needs for expression rather than being concerned with the needs of the person receiving the communication.

The first step in active communication is to attune yourself to the needs of the person with whom you want to communicate. That person's level of understanding, attitudes, and relationship with you affects the reception of your messages.

Other factors deserving preparatory attention before communicating are time and place. Sufficient time should be allocated for the communication. Some issues can be worked through rapidly, but more time and attention are needed for dealing effectively with issues that are complex and personal. Since the physical setting makes a good deal of difference, locating your conversations appropriately can add tremendously to their quality.

Check the receptiveness of the other person. This can be done quite openly by asking, "Have you got time to listen to me on this topic?" Thereby an agreement is made, and the conversation is identified as important.

Briefly identifying the purpose of the session is helpful prior to methodically and clearly going through the content. The speaker should watch for nonverbal signals that his communication is being received. A more direct check on how the message is coming across is done by inviting comment or questions. Sometimes it is helpful to show visually the information or idea being described and to use this visualization as a focus for discussion.

Presenters who show a low level of competence in their communications with others have several of the following characteristics:

- Inappropriate timing in conversations;
- Unclear definitions of the purpose of the conversation;
- Repetitive and wordy inputs;

- Insufficient checking for understanding;
- Lack of purpose and rambling style of conversation;
- Critical and argumentative reaction.

Block 3. Lack of Open Expression

Much creativity stems from the discontent of people who perceive that present systems, methods, and products are inadequate. From their critical evaluation comes the energy to initiate change.

People often speak as though openness were easily achieved, but this is untrue. Although some kinds of open expression, for example giving praise, can be readily practiced, it is much more difficult to be open about matters that seem to be unconstructive, improper, or blocked. Many people find it difficult to be open about negative aspects, especially to the people responsible for the status quo. For this reason, their criticisms are muted and generalized, thereby losing impact.

Unexpressed decisions are made every day by people who limit the extent to which they are open and restrain how they express themselves. They need to develop the capacity to be more open more often. If this is not done, energy gets blocked within the person, who then is unable to experience a sense of self-responsibility. Without this sense of being responsible, much of the potential strength and power of people remain undeveloped and their creativity is stunted. Openness should be supported and strengthened; it needs to be valued for its own sake.

Someone who is attempting to be more open about genuine problems often will say, "I don't know where to begin." Our answer to this is "Begin anywhere. Just talk and we can make sense of it later." Out of the expression of difficulty and the emotions that go with it can come new energy, which has the capacity to solve problems and manage progress.

Block 4. Inadequate Techniques

Applied creativity is partly discipline and technique. Since most creative techniques are relatively straightforward, they are, unfortunately, scorned by many. However, the following three methods have helped us considerably:

BRAINSTORMING

Brainstorming is a well-known group approach that gains its strength from separating the process of generating ideas from the process of evaluating them. It has the capacity to generate a large quantity of ideas rapidly. These can be sifted later for merit. (See Activity 40, "Team Brainstorming.")

MIND MAPS

Mind maps are most easily read by those who prepare them and offer a creative and rapid tool for generating ideas. This technique, developed by Tony Buzan,[3] can speed progress in acquiring, collating, and structuring information by helping to:

- Prevent ideas from getting lost;
- Stimulate individual/group creativity;
- Decrease unnecessary repetition;
- Increase interest among group members;
- Clarify links between ideas;
- Show areas of insufficient information.

The diagram shown in Figure 6 is an example of how one individual made a personal assessment of the uses of the mind-map approach. It contains the main points and uses of the mind map. Key words are used to catch the essence of ideas and relationships and key points can be seen quickly. Colors may be used to add further emphasis.

As you can see, the mind map contains an enormous amount of information arranged in ways that enable the brain to readily comprehend the patterns, key ideas, and easily extend understanding.

WHY/HOW

One of the most interesting problem-solving techniques yet developed is known as the Why/How chart. This is described in Activity 28, "Why/How Charting."

The Why/How chart combines the brainstorming and mind-map techniques with a third idea, termed tiers of objectives. It readily can be observed that some statements of direction are very general and broad, such as "improve the quality of the environment," while other statements are specific and concrete, such as "clean the green slime off the water fountain in the park once a month." The relationship between these direction statements is shown in Figure 7. This is relevant to the creative process because innovation requires that all the tiers of objectives be considered. Attempting simply to work at the level of broad aims is insufficient and concentrating on specific activities can mean that one "does not see the forest for the trees."

---

[3]Tony Buzan, *Use Your Head.* London: BBC Publications, 1974.

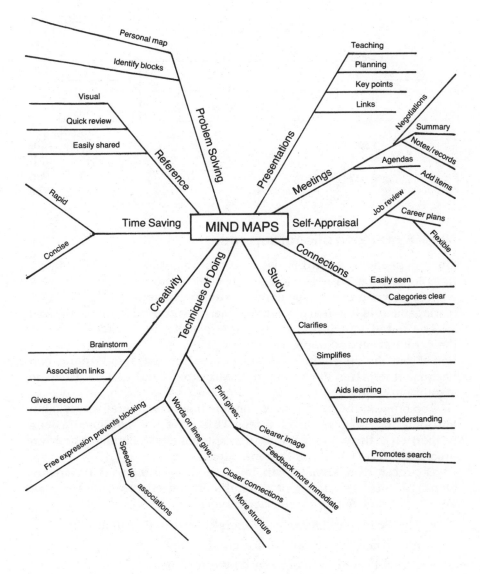

Figure 6. An example of a mind map.

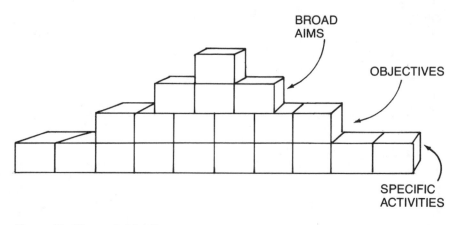

Figure 7. Tiers of objectives

Block 5. Organizational Support

Much depends on a hard-to-define corporate attitude towards innovation. Some organizations manage to become exciting places in which to work, and when this happens much vitality is available. A key task of management is to release the latent energy available in the work force.

The bored repetition of meaningless tasks by workers increases their frustration and depresses their vitality, enthusiasm, and innovation. From the viewpoint of organizational health, this is dangerous because it deprives the system of creative potential and increases resistance to change.

Too often in the past, innovation has been considered a rare talent and only was required from a few. This error has hardened a large proportion of the working population against novelty and has deprived organizations of countless valuable ideas.

Organizational support can be a valuable aid to taking creative steps, despite their inherent difficulty. To be effective, this support should have the following characteristics:

- The individual knows that others believe in the value of his work.
- Ideas, not the person, are criticized.
- Difficulties are actively heard by colleagues.
- Adequate resources for testing are provided.
- The individual is not punished if things go wrong.

When an organization gives support to creativity, creative effort can spread very widely. For example, while the executive team develops new strategies, operator groups are considering alternative ways of performing a task. Not all jobs have an equal opportunity for creativity, but all have a creative aspect.

SUGGESTED ACTIVITIES FOR BLOCKAGE / GENERATOR XI:
CREATIVE CAPACITY

Activity Number & Title

40. Team Brainstorming
41. Creative Change
42. Creative Presentation

XII. Intergroup Relationships

REVIEW QUESTIONS

12. Conflicts between our team and other groups are quite common.
24. Our team does not have constructive relationships with some of the other teams within the organization.
36. The team does not respond sufficiently to the needs of other teams in the organization.
48. We do not actively seek to develop our working relationships with other teams.
60. Some significant mistakes would have been avoided if we had better communication with other teams.
72. In this organization, teams and departments tend to compete rather than collaborate.
84. Some of the other teams/departments seem to have a low opinion of us.
96. We do not get to know the people working in other teams in the organization.
108. If we worked better with other teams, it would help us all to be more effective.

Teams usually have to relate to individuals and groups outside their own boundaries. We often watch groups developing impressions and images of each other that go beyond logical assessments; e.g., one group is called "slipshod," another is "arrogant," and a third is "weak." Industrial psychologists who have observed this process of stereotyping report that people tend to accept their stereotype as truth and act from this basis.

COMPETITION

Groups frequently engage in competition that may be disguised but rarely is irrelevant. Although much energy and concern are invested in maintaining an intergroup competition, it often is difficult to detect because the competitiveness is a subtle undercurrent, expressed obliquely and indirectly.

Managers often talk about their jobs in terms borrowed from sport. They speak of "playing to win," "scoring points," and identifying "the name of the game." Such expressions reveal how people think about their jobs and what mental pictures help them to interpret what happens.

Children are inculcated with images of "winning," "smashing the opposition," and "being the champions," which persist into adult life. When such attitudes are struck between teams within an organization, they set up "win-lose" relationships with each other. When one team strives to win at the expense of the other, the results are costly: the withdrawal of communication and close relationships and the downgrading of contributions, without considering the costs for the organization as a whole.

Teams almost always are arranged in a hierarchy, and those that are higher in the structure often find it difficult to obtain good, clear, and open communication from those below. When senior teams cast their role as arbiters, inquisitors, and angels of retribution, the subordinate teams quickly learn to cover their tracks and defend their territory.

DEVELOPING INTERGROUP RELATIONS

Teams may regard each other benignly, but they still fail to develop depth of communication. Here the fault lies with mechanics rather than attitude because the groups may have few spontaneous means of interrelating. A conscious effort should be made to develop intergroup relations and work through overall objectives and the minutiae of routine contact.

Deliberately improving intergroup relationships involves conscious planning and creating opportunities that often do not exist naturally in day-to-day organizational life. The process for improving blocked intergroup relationships includes the following steps.

Step 1. Identifying the Common Objective

Groups often are hazy about the objectives and output from other units within the organization. Although an objective such as "to make more profit" would be readily accepted as a common aim of the different parts of an organization, this is far too superficial to be useful. Objectives should be explicit and worked through in considerable detail.

Teams should become genuinely conscious of their dependence on other groups within their organization. The sharing of objectives and the identifying of overlaps and differences are so crucial that without these processes, relationships often degenerate into formal sniping via memoranda or indifference.

Step 2. Personal Understanding

There is no substitute for relating personally to individuals who are in other groups. With personal knowledge there is much more readiness to contact informally and to think of the others while making decisions. The need for personal contact becomes greater when a possibility of conflict exists.

Group members need to feel that they understand the motivation and driving forces of the members of the other group. One departmental head, speaking of his relations with another department, put it this way, "After our meeting, I felt that we understood you much more as people; we understood your motives and felt sympathy for you. How we could help you and how you could help us became clear. We needed the information about who you are, how you work, and whether you actually do what you say you will do. Once these questions were answered, all the rest fell together."

Step 3. Developing Mechanisms for Relationships

Most large organizations do not have sufficient avenues for working through intergroup issues and problems. In this respect, organizations are frequently immature, and they need mechanisms that enable high quality communication and interaction between different departments. Before such avenues can be created, the need for them must be felt and some resources allocated to meeting this need. Before creating the means to bridge the inevitable gaps between groups, it helps to assess systematically the needs of each group involved.

Step 4. Managing the Boundary

It often happens that one or two people represent their team in relation to other groups. The selection and briefing of these representatives is of great importance because the other group frequently forms its views of a team from its representatives and negotiating style.

Step 5. Building a Climate of Trust

Trust is based on people disclosing information about their intentions and methods. Most significantly, trust is built between people when they work through difficult situations together and each has the opportunity to assess the other. Groups that want to develop an open and trusting relationshp with other groups will have to expose both their strengths and their weaknesses. They will demonstrate that they are prepared to face difficult issues and work them through. They also will try to be consistent and follow through on the actions they undertake.

A CASE STUDY

Experience has taught us that intergroup relationships readily can be improved in most organizations, and with substantial potential benefits; however, many managers lack the necessary skills. They fail to develop constructive relationships outside their boundaries that could reap a plentiful harvest.

We know a good example of such a problem that occurred in a food manufacturing business. A large department (A) was converting basic raw materials into a partly-finished product, which then was passed on to another process unit (B) for conversion into the final packaged goods.

The company hired a new factory manager who was intent on cost reduction. After reviewing the objectives of department A, the new manager set some stiff cost-reduction targets for that department.

The departmental manager gathered his supervisors around him and explained the situation. Since the department's biggest cost item was raw materials, he suggested a drive to save raw materials and cut tolerances to the bone. The supervisors, who were old hands and respected their boss, set to work with a will. After three months, savings of nearly $100,000 had been made. The departmental team members congratulated themselves on their success and started making plans for spending their fat merit raises.

It was also at this three-month stage that the factory manager started hearing complaints from department B, down the line, that their reject rate was rocketing, due to defective and underweight raw materials.

At the end of the six-month period, the first department had met its cost-reduction targets and had saved over $300,000. But during the year-end review of the plant's overall results, it was found that the losses due to rejection and rework in department B had exceeded $400,000, and the plant as a whole had lost some $100,000. The first department had "won" as far as its team goals were concerned, but as a consequence, the second department and the plant both had lost.

Management teams often need clear signals from outside the group to let them know that they are "on the track." This applies most strongly to teams that provide services to other parts of an organization.

KEY IDEAS

The following ideas are the basis for a theory of interteam relations:

1. Organizations can be likened to living organisms.

2. The whole organism or system may be made up of a series of parts. Each part has a function to play in the overall working of the total system.

3. If a particular part of the system is internally defective, this will have a damaging effect on the whole organism.

4. If the parts are not sympathetic to each other, and do not play complementary roles, the organism as a whole will suffer. If this malaise is serious, the organism as a whole may break up and cease to exist.

5. A key factor in maintaining a healthy total organism is for the boundaries that exist between its parts to remain open, allowing the exchange of signals and information between the parts. If the boundaries are closed, the whole organism will wither and possibly die.

Some teams can become so fascinated by working on their internal functions that the state of their boundaries becomes a matter of low concern. This can become a morbid condition, particularly when teams deliberately close their boundaries with other groups in an organization and escalate competition to disadvantage rival teams.

SUGGESTED ACTIVITIES FOR BLOCKAGE / GENERATOR XII:
INTERGROUP RELATIONSHIPS

Activity Number & Title

43. Organizational Mirror
44. Circles of Influence
45. Castles in the Air
46. Cartoon Time

Building Strengths and Clearing Blockages

Tools for Team Building

This part of the book is concerned with action. Here we describe forty-six projects that have proved useful in other team-building programs.

The chief skill in managing change is "knowing the right thing to do next." However, it is impossible for us to provide a fool-proof set of instructions to fit your particular situation because a group's needs can only be assessed from within. Therefore, we ask you to thoroughly examine each of the projects and determine which ones meet your group's needs at this time.

Our experience has revealed that teams find at least half of these activities valuable, but teams never consistently like the same activities. For example, one team finds that Activity 6, "Stages of Team Development," leads to much useful discussion. Another team fails to find much relevance in the same project. Only you and your team can exercise the necessary discrimination in choice.

DESIGNING A TEAM-BUILDING PROGRAM

One of the advantages of using the project approach to team building is being able to assemble a program to suit your particular needs. However, there is a risk that trying one project after another can fragment your efforts. To avoid this, we suggest that your team select and plan a sequence of three or more projects. Their participation in the process increases the members' commitment to the program. Their understanding of their experience in the program also can be increased by taking an hour for a team review when the initial program of activities has been completed.

Off-Site Team Building

Team building often is best conducted away from the day-to-day pressures of work. An off-site team-building meeting offers an opportunity for a methodical review and creative and relaxed planning. Such a meeting can be constructed using the following guidelines:

1. Plan the schedule with the following formula in mind: each extra day of the meeting approximately doubles its value to the participants up to a total of four days.

2. Meet with your team prior to an off-site meeting to establish objectives for the meeting and to determine how you can measure its progress.

3. Choose a sequence of projects that meet your objectives, beginning with the more straightforward activities. Use the time periods suggested in the activities to construct a schedule for the meeting.

4. Employ a skilled team-building consultant when the team is moving into uncharted waters or is dealing with complicated interpersonal problems.

5. Arrange for facilities that ensure against interruptions in the team's working sessions.

6. Enjoy yourselves.

Choosing the Activities

On the following pages is an activity index, which gives the title of each activity, indicates any team blockage to which it relates, and briefly describes the objectives of the activity. Each activity is also given a symbolic rating. As a rule of thumb, the ratings indicate the following:

Symbol	Explanation of Rating
*	Straightforward projects that can be built into normal team operations with no special preparation or outside help.
**	Activities that may raise sensitive or interpersonal issues. Before entering into these activities, the team should review them and obtain the voluntary agreement of all members to do them.

***   More advanced projects that are likely to bring out sensitive issues affecting the whole team or individual members.

Before entering into these projects, the team should carefully review them and obtain the voluntary agreement of all members to do them. It also is useful for the team members to consider two questions:

1. Are we ready to face possibly sensitive personal issues in the team?

2. Would the risks be reduced if we used a skilled external agent to help us work through the sensitive issues? (See "The Team-Development Consultant" in Part 1.)

O   Activities that entail the giving or receiving of personal feedback. Before a team begins any of these activities, it is suggested that the team undertake and review Activity 1, "Giving Feedback."

USING THE ACTIVITIES

The following guidelines may help you to use the activities successfully:

1. When selecting activities, read the activity index and particularly note the "Rating" column.

2. As a team, review all the activities before selecting several that you want to attempt. List these in order of priority.

3. Begin by examining the projects that work on the key blockages identified by the results of your Team-Review Questionnaire. (The activity index indicates the relationships between team blockages and corrective activities.)

4. Since each activity has detailed step-by-step instructions, the person who will lead the activity should preview it. Preplanning usually is necessary for the success of the event. The group will need a private room that is quiet, free from distractions, and adequately ventilated. Everyone should be comfortably seated and tables should be provided if necessary for the activity. The standard means of recording and displaying information is writing with colored

felt-tipped marking pens on a blank flip chart or a large pad of newsprint paper that is sitting on an easel. This allows the leader to tear off charts and affix them to the wall with masking tape for group reference.

5. When using an activity, adhere to the framework suggested whenever possible because it provides a useful discipline.

6. Allow sufficient time for participants to discuss the experience after completing an activity in order for feelings to be expressed and uncertainties resolved.

7. Ensure against the occurrence of interruptions during team-building sessions.

What To Do When: An Activity Index

Activity Number	Title	Rating	Use with This Team Blockage	Objectives
1	Giving Feedback	O*	General Introductory Activity	To help a team establish its own "rules" for giving personal feedback. *This activity is considered a prerequisite to activities with an O rating.*
2	Setting Team-Building Objectives	*	General Activity	To clarify a team's development needs. To set objectives for team development and criteria for its success. To provide a framework for beginning a team-building program.
3	Designing an Off-Site Meeting	*		To allow team members to define the objectives and design the content of an off-site meeting. To plan how to successfully manage the event.
4	Planning for Appraisal and Counseling	O**	General Activity	To provide a systematic checklist for any person to review before conducting a formal appraisal or counseling session.
5	Team Problem Solving: The Zin Obelisk	*	General Activity	To experience and examine the sharing of information in team problem solving. To study leadership, cooperation, and conflict issues in team problem solving. To develop team problem-solving skills.

Activity Number	Title	Rating	Use with This Team Blockage	Objectives
6	Stages of Team Development	**	General Activity	To provide a framework for a team to evaluate its current stage of development. To choose and set priorities for activities to be undertaken to enhance a team's development.
7	Defining Leadership Style: A Sharing Activity	O**	I. Effective Leadership	To help the team and the team manager understand and clarify the manager's leadership style. To help the team members give feedback to the team leader.
8	The Best Leaders I Have Known	O**	I. Effective Leadership	To help team members define positive leadership characteristics and share these definitions with the team leader.
9	Who Performs the Leadership Functions?	O**	I. Effective Leadership	To help a team understand how leadership functions are currently carried out in the team. To determine the best ways of carrying out leadership functions in the future.
10	Negotiating the Team Manager's Role	O***	I. Effective Leadership	To clarify the team manager's expectations of the team and the team members' expectations of their manager. To identify significant differences in these expectations.
11	Team Skills Audit	O**	II. Suitable Membership	To identify the social and technical skills required by the team. To evaluate the team's present skills. To select the skill areas most in need of development. *This requires a substantial investment of time and effort.*

Activity Number	Title	Rating	Use with This Team Blockage	Objectives
12	Selecting a New Team Member	*	II. Suitable Membership	To help a team develop a consensual approach to selecting a new member of the team, and in particular define: 1. The specific nature of the job to be filled; 2. The in-team relationships of a new job holder; 3. The main skills required; 4. The kind of person the members would like for the job.
13	Use Us, We're the Best	**	II. Suitable Membership	To critically review the skills, capabilities, and potential of a team. To evaluate the marketability of a team.
14	Test Your Commitment	*	II. Team Commitment	To help a team identify factors that increase or decrease the level of members' commitment (positive identification with the team and its objectives).
15	Increasing Team Commitment: An Adventure Project	**	III. Team Commitment	To acquaint and involve team members with one another in more depth. To develop informal ties between team members. To increase the members' feelings of commitment to the team.
16	Team Counseling	O***	III. Team Commitment	To explore an individual member's feelings about his relationships with the team. To mobilize the support and skills of the team in helping individuals develop their relationships within the group.

Activity Number	Title	Rating	Use with This Team Blockage	Objectives
17	The Commitment Problem	*	III. Team Commitment	To examine individual and team motivation and commitment by analyzing the role play of a specific managerial problem.
18	Team-Climate Questionnaire	O**	IV. Team Climate	To help a team examine its working climate and prepare an action plan for improving it.
19	From Me to You, From You to Me	O***	IV. Team Climate	To provide team members with a structured and practical means of giving feedback to one another. To help team members work through problems in personal and work relationships.
20	Cave Rescue	*	IV. Team Climate	To examine the impact of individual value and attitudes on group decision making. To study problem-solving procedures in groups. To practice consensus-seeking behavior.
21	Defining the Team's Maintenance and Achievement Activities	*	V. Team Achievement	To enable each team member to classify his work activities and the time allocated to them under the categories of maintenance or achievement. To analyze the whole team's work activities and time allocations, determine whether they are sufficient and, if not, plan changes.
22	Identifying Team Success	*	V. Team Achievement	To examine the past activity of a team. To evaluate and chart the successes and failures of a team. To use the evaluation information in predicting a team's future effectiveness.

Activity Number	Title	Rating	Use with This Team Blockage	Objectives
23	New Game	*	V. Team Achievement	To examine the dynamics of a team's performance in producing a tangible result within a short time period. To observe the effect of feedback on team performance.
24	Organizational Role	*	VI. Corporate Role	To assist a team in defining its role in an organization and the ways in which it relates to other significant groups. *This activity is particularly relevant to teams that act in a support or service capacity.*
25	Mapping the Organization	*	VI. Corporate Role	To define a team's position within its organization and with the other parts of the organization to which it relates. To define the nature of those relationships.
26	Team Survival	*	VI. Corporate Role	To clarify the essential reasons for the existence of a specific team as a part of the wider organization.
27	How Good Are Your Meetings?	*	VII. Work Methods	To diagnose the problems a team has with the planning and control of its meetings. To plan and take specific actions to overcome these problems.
28	Why/How Charting	*	VII. Work Methods	To help a team clarify its objectives and plan appropriate problem-solving actions.
29	Effective Problem-Solving Survey	O**	VII. Work Methods	To identify strengths and weaknesses in team problem solving. To set agendas for strengthening the weakest characteristics.

Activity Number	Title	Rating	Use with This Team Blockage	Objectives
30	Team's Mission and Individual Objectives	**	VIII. Team Organization	To test for strengths or problems in the ways that team members relate their individual goals to the team's overall mission. To help clarify the team's mission to team members.
31	Team Communications	O**	VIII. Team Organization	To identify specific malfunctions in team communication. To plan actions to correct the team-communication malfunctions.
32	Start Up	*	VIII. Team Organization	To examine different work roles and methods of organization. To observe how each member's contribution fits into the team's overall effort.
33	How Do We Make Decisions?	**	VIII. Team Organization	To examine how team and individual members typically make decisions. To plan changes in the team's decision-making process.
34	Like and Don't Like	**	IX. Critiquing	To help a team initiate a critical appraisal of its own functioning. To allow team members to define their basic likes and dislikes about the team. To plan actions for strengthening the positive and changing the negative team characteristics.

Activity Number	Title	Rating	Use with This Team Blockage	Objectives
35	The Best and the Worst	*	IX. Critiquing	To look back and identify the best and the worst aspects of the team's performance over a specific period. To identify and share ideas on why these aspects existed. To develop team consensus on future actions to reinforce the positive and overcome the negative features of the team's operation.
36	You Should Have Been a...	O**	IX. Critiquing	To facilitate the sharing of constructive feedback between team members.
37	Is It OK To Be More Me?	O**	X. Individual Development	To assist an individual in identifying: 1. What kinds of past influences affect his behavior; and 2. Whether he wants to change any aspects of his current behavior patterns.
38	Managing People Skills Inventory	**	X. Individual Development	To provide a systematic basis for a manager's self-evaluation and for team feedback on individual managerial skills. To identify priorities for individual development of managerial skills.
39	Good Coaching Practice	*	X. Individual Development	To identify the skills of good coaching practice. To allow a group to set standards for its own performance.
40	Team Brainstorming	*	XI. Creative Capacity	To practice a means of generating ideas. To develop skills in creative problem solving.

Activity Number	Title	Rating	Use with This Team Blockage	Objectives
41	Creative Change	*	XI. Creative Capacity	To study the stages in a creative process. To use the creative process to accomplish real benefits for the team.
42	Creative Presentation	*	XI. Creative Capacity	To help group members identify the creative strengths of their team and themselves. To study how team members work together on a problem-solving task.
43	Organizational Mirror	O**	XII. Intergroup Relationships	To bring two teams together for mutual and self-analysis. To help the teams share these perceptions. To suggest changes or developments that would be beneficial to joint effectiveness.
44	Circles of Influence	*	XII. Intergroup Relationships	To use a systematic approach to evaluate the forces influencing a team and to plan ways to increase its strength and influence.
45	Castles in the Air	**	XII. Intergroup Relationships	To experience group problem solving. To explore relationships between groups. To investigate management style.
46	Cartoon Time	*	XII. Intergroup Relationships	To experience the intergroup dynamics involved in the accomplishment of a creative task. To assess the individual and group behaviors that helped to accomplish a creative task (functional behaviors) or hindered successful accomplishment (dysfunctional behaviors).

1 Giving Feedback

Purpose

To help a team establish its own "rules" for giving personal feedback.

Time

Approximately one hour.

Materials

I.   A copy each of the Giving Feedback Statement Sheet and the Giving Feedback Ranking Sheet and a pencil for each participant.

II. A large newsprint pad and felt-tipped markers, or a chalkboard and chalk.

Background

Some activities in this section involve team members in giving feedback to one another. The giving and receiving of feedback is one of the most significant ways of assisting personal growth. When asked to identify some of the most important experiences in their personal development, most people will reflect for a few moments and then talk about particular people who have given them direct and pertinent information about themselves. Such feedback can have so much impact that it can profoundly influence the ways in which people behave. However, as with many powerful tools, feedback can be abused, and sometimes people are hurt or deflated through receiving feedback. Since the intention behind giving feedback should never be to damage or hurt, ways should be found for giving feedback that result in the person being stronger and more effective.

This activity enables a team to evaluate its approach to giving and receiving feedback and, therefore, it is a prerequisite for later activities that entail a significant element of giving and receiving personal feedback. These activities are identified by the symbol O in the activity index.

Method

I. The leader distributes a Giving Feedback Statement Sheet, a Giving Feedback Ranking Sheet, and a pencil to each team member and instructs each of them to do the following:

1. Pick out the five statements that are most significant to you in giving feedback and list them on the Ranking Sheet, giving brief reasons for the importance of each statement to you.

2. Present your five priority statements to the group and briefly state why each one is important to you.

II. The leader lists the numbers of each person's priority statements on the newsprint pad and helps the team decide through discussion which priority statements are most significant and which ones they would like to omit, if any.

III. After the group agrees about a final list, the leader charts it under the heading:

For this team, good feedback is:

1. _____

2. _____

etc.

IV. Before using any other activities that involve giving feedback, this "good feedback is . . ." list should be displayed and reviewed.

GIVING FEEDBACK STATEMENT SHEET

Useful feedback is:

1. *Given with Care.* To be useful, feedback requires the giver to feel concern for and to care for the person receiving feedback — to want to help, not hurt the other person.

2. *Given with Attention.* It is important to pay attention to what you are doing as you give feedback. This helps you to engage in a two-way exchange with some depth of communication.

3. *Invited by the Recipient.* Feedback is most effective when the receiver has invited the comments. This provides a platform for openness and some guidelines; and it also gives the receiver an opportunity to identify and explore particular areas of concern.

4. *Directly Expressed.* Good feedback is specific and deals clearly with particular incidents and behavior. Pussy-footing or making vague and wooly statements is of little value. The most useful help is direct, open, and concrete.

5. *Fully Expressed.* Effective feedback requires more than a bald statement of facts. Feelings also need to be expressed so that the receiver can judge the full impact of his behavior.

6. *Uncluttered by Evaluative Judgments.* Often it is helpful not to give feedback composed of judgments or evaluations. If you wish to offer judgments, then it is necessary to state clearly that these are matters of subjective evaluation and then to simply describe the situation as you see it and let the person concerned make the evaluation.

7. *Well Timed.* The most useful feedback is given when the receiver is receptive to it and is sufficiently close to the particular event being discussed for it to be fresh in his mind. Storing comments can lead to a build-up of recriminations and reduces the effectiveness of feedback when it is finally given.

8. *Readily Actionable.* The most useful feedback centers around behavior that can be changed by the receiver. Feedback concerning matters outside the control of the receiver is less useful. It often is helpful to suggest alternative ways of behaving that allow the receiver to think about new ways of tackling old problems.

9. *Checked and Clarified.* If possible, feedback should be checked out with other people to explore whether one person's perceptions are shared by others. This is especially useful in a training group and also can be promoted in a work team. Different viewpoints can be collected and assimilated, points of difference and similarity clarified, and a more objective picture developed.

GIVING FEEDBACK RANKING SHEET

1. Statement and number	Why I think it is important
2.	
3.	
4.	
5.	

② Setting Team-Building Objectives

Purpose

I. To clarify a team's development needs.

II. To set objectives for team-development progress and criteria for its success.

III. To provide a framework for beginning a team-building program.

Time

Approximately two hours.

Materials

I. A copy of the Team-Review Questionnaire, the Team-Review Questionnaire Answer Sheet, and the Team-Review Questionnaire Interpretation Sheet (all these materials may be found in Part 2) for each participant.

II. A large newsprint pad, felt-tipped markers and masking tape, or a chalkboard and chalk.

III. Blank paper and a pencil for each participant.

Method

I. The leader (or coordinator) distributes to each team member the materials required for completion of the Team-Review Questionnaire.

II. Team members are directed to read the instructions and complete the questionnaire.

III. After the members have completed the Team-Review Questionnaire, each participant is instructed to write the three blockages that he feels to be most important. (See the Team-Review Interpretation Sheet.)

IV. At this point, the leader asks the team members whether they wish to express any concerns about the likely outcomes of the questionnaire. All their concerns are listed on the newsprint and discussed until team members voluntarily express a willingness to proceed. Should anxieties remain, we suggest that the leader close the session and call in an external consultant to help the team proceed.

V.   Following the team's agreement to proceed, the lists of priority blocks (from Step III) are submitted anonymously to the leader.

VI. The leader posts the scores (see the Team-Review Questionnaire Analysis) and leads a discussion of the scores using the following questions as aids:

1. How far do the survey results accurately mirror our team's current position?

2. Is it important that we work on developing our team?

VII. At an appropriate point in the discussion, the leader sets the task of reaching consensus on which blockage the team wants to work on within the next two months.

VIII. Each of the team members is asked to spend ten minutes in completing the following statement:

We will know that we are making progress in clearing this blockage when:

IX. Each member's contributions are charted (anonymously, if preferred) and discussed. After reviewing each member's success criteria for the blockage, the team produces a list of criteria, or objectives. If there is any difficulty in clarifying objectives or methods of tackling agreed objectives, the team can use the Why/How approach described in Activity 28, "Why/How Charting."

X.   The team then appoints one or two people to study the list, research possible actions for achieving the criteria, and return to the team with a suggested program for working on the chosen blockage.

③ Designing an Off-Site Meeting

Purpose

I. To allow team members to define the objectives and design the content of an off-site meeting.

II. To plan how to successfully manage the event.

Time

A total of four hours.

Materials

I. A large newsprint pad and felt-tipped markers, or a chalkboard and chalk.

II. Blank paper and a pencil for each participant.

Physical Arrangement

A room that is large enough to accommodate the entire team, with space (or separate rooms) for subgroups to meet separately.

Method

PART ONE

I. After convening a two-hour meeting of the team, the leader distributes paper and a pencil to each member. He instructs each member to identify two or three problems confronting the team at this time and write them, privately, on a slip of paper. (Approximately ten minutes.)

II. The leader collects the papers and lists the problems on a chalkboard or the newsprint pad.

III. The group looks for any clear categories that emerge from the list and assigns a priority to each problem, using the following key:

3 = Crucial

2 = Important

1 = Slight

0 = Insignificant

(Approximately fifteen minutes.)

IV. The group considers the degree of seriousness of its common problems and estimates how much it would be prepared to spend to solve the problems. (Fifteen minutes.)

V. The team considers the degree of complexity inherent in the problems identified and tries to estimate (approximately) the amount of time that it might take to solve each problem. After this discussion, the members assign a time-factor number to each problem, using the following scale:

3 = Very complex (more than one day to resolve)

2 = Complex (about one-half day to resolve)

1 = Straightforward (less than one hour)

0 = Simple (a few minutes)

(Fifteen minutes.)

VI. The leader completes the following table, listing the scores for each category and totaling them. (Approximately ten minutes.)

PROBLEM	IMPORTANCE	COMPLEXITY	TOTAL

VII. Using the table, the team determines the amount of time that is convenient and useful to spend on its off-site meeting. The leader can note as a rule of thumb that the value of the meeting to participants doubles with each additional day up to a total of four days.

VIII. The leader divides the team into pairs (dyads) or threes (triads) and assigns each subgroup the task of reviewing the activities in this book and designing an off-site meeting. Each subgroup arranges to meet following the meeting to develop its plans. (Twenty minutes.)

PART TWO

I.   When all the subgroups have completed the assignment, the leader reconvenes the whole team for a one-hour meeting.

II.   Each subgroup presents its plan and rationale.

III. The total group discusses each plan and either chooses one approach or designs a synthesis of favored ideas.

IV.   One person is appointed to arrange the event. This involves arranging the practical details, seeing that materials are available, and coordinating the projects.

V.   If the team feels that it lacks the experience to handle the meeting, an external catalyst or consultant can be useful. (See "The Team-Development Consultant" in Part 1.)

4 Planning for Appraisal and Counseling

Purpose

To provide a systematic check list for any person to review before conducting a formal appraisal or counseling session.

Method

I. Set time aside to use the Counseling Process Chart at least two weeks before the date of the appraisal or counseling session.

II. Read quickly through the process chart *up to the section marked Interview Start,* noting any significant points that you respond to negatively and marking each of these with no.

III. Go back to each of the items that you have marked no and consider the following questions:

   1. What do I have to do to change the no to a yes?
   2. Can I achieve this change by myself or do I have to use other courses (discussion with other managers, formal training, etc.)?

IV. Read the remainder of the process sheet (after the Interview-Start point) and note any points that you feel may be of particular significance. Arrange these notes into a check list to use during the forthcoming interview.

V. After the interview, compare the check list with the whole Counseling Process Chart and note any points that could be improved the next time you conduct an appraisal or counseling interview.

COUNSELING PROCESS CHART

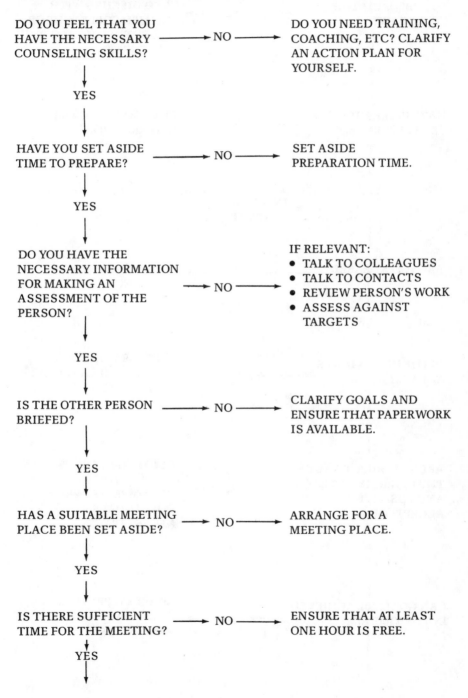

DO YOU FEEL THAT YOU HAVE THE NECESSARY COUNSELING SKILLS? ——→ NO ——→ DO YOU NEED TRAINING, COACHING, ETC? CLARIFY AN ACTION PLAN FOR YOURSELF.

YES

HAVE YOU SET ASIDE TIME TO PREPARE? ——→ NO ——→ SET ASIDE PREPARATION TIME.

YES

DO YOU HAVE THE NECESSARY INFORMATION FOR MAKING AN ASSESSMENT OF THE PERSON? ——→ NO ——→ IF RELEVANT:
- TALK TO COLLEAGUES
- TALK TO CONTACTS
- REVIEW PERSON'S WORK
- ASSESS AGAINST TARGETS

YES

IS THE OTHER PERSON BRIEFED? ——→ NO ——→ CLARIFY GOALS AND ENSURE THAT PAPERWORK IS AVAILABLE.

YES

HAS A SUITABLE MEETING PLACE BEEN SET ASIDE? ——→ NO ——→ ARRANGE FOR A MEETING PLACE.

YES

IS THERE SUFFICIENT TIME FOR THE MEETING? ——→ NO ——→ ENSURE THAT AT LEAST ONE HOUR IS FREE.

YES

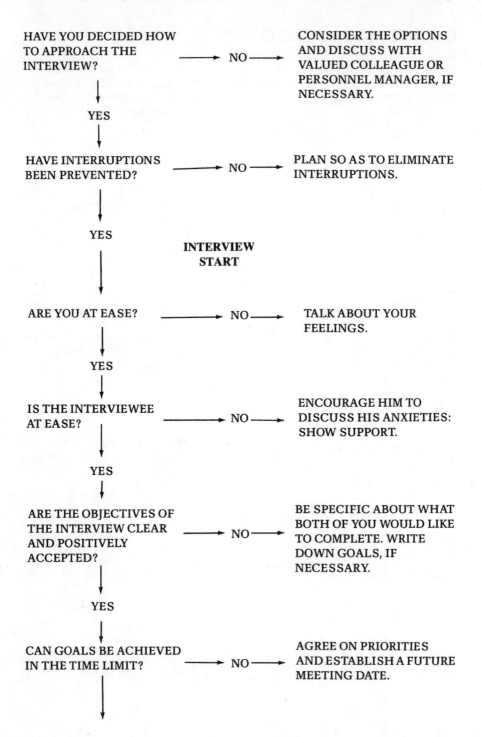

HAVE YOU DECIDED HOW TO APPROACH THE INTERVIEW? —— NO ——> CONSIDER THE OPTIONS AND DISCUSS WITH VALUED COLLEAGUE OR PERSONNEL MANAGER, IF NECESSARY.

YES

HAVE INTERRUPTIONS BEEN PREVENTED? —— NO ——> PLAN SO AS TO ELIMINATE INTERRUPTIONS.

YES

INTERVIEW START

ARE YOU AT EASE? —— NO ——> TALK ABOUT YOUR FEELINGS.

YES

IS THE INTERVIEWEE AT EASE? —— NO ——> ENCOURAGE HIM TO DISCUSS HIS ANXIETIES: SHOW SUPPORT.

YES

ARE THE OBJECTIVES OF THE INTERVIEW CLEAR AND POSITIVELY ACCEPTED? —— NO ——> BE SPECIFIC ABOUT WHAT BOTH OF YOU WOULD LIKE TO COMPLETE. WRITE DOWN GOALS, IF NECESSARY.

YES

CAN GOALS BE ACHIEVED IN THE TIME LIMIT? —— NO ——> AGREE ON PRIORITIES AND ESTABLISH A FUTURE MEETING DATE.

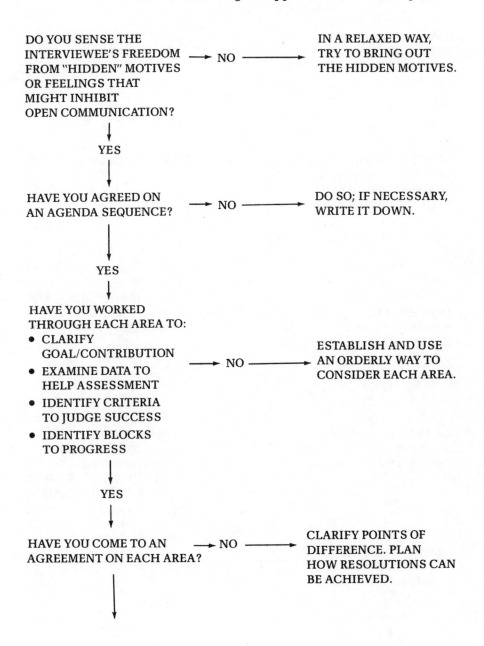

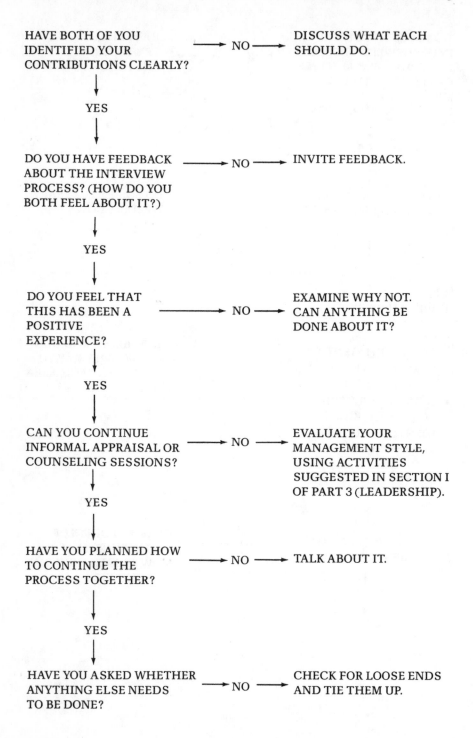

HAVE BOTH OF YOU
IDENTIFIED YOUR ——→ NO ——→ DISCUSS WHAT EACH
CONTRIBUTIONS CLEARLY?   SHOULD DO.

YES

DO YOU HAVE FEEDBACK
ABOUT THE INTERVIEW ——→ NO ——→ INVITE FEEDBACK.
PROCESS? (HOW DO YOU
BOTH FEEL ABOUT IT?)

YES

DO YOU FEEL THAT   EXAMINE WHY NOT.
THIS HAS BEEN A ——→ NO ——→ CAN ANYTHING BE
POSITIVE   DONE ABOUT IT?
EXPERIENCE?

YES

CAN YOU CONTINUE   EVALUATE YOUR
INFORMAL APPRAISAL OR ——→ NO ——→ MANAGEMENT STYLE,
COUNSELING SESSIONS?   USING ACTIVITIES
                                     SUGGESTED IN SECTION I
                                     OF PART 3 (LEADERSHIP).

YES

HAVE YOU PLANNED HOW
TO CONTINUE THE ——→ NO ——→ TALK ABOUT IT.
PROCESS TOGETHER?

YES

HAVE YOU ASKED WHETHER   CHECK FOR LOOSE ENDS
ANYTHING ELSE NEEDS ——→ NO ——→ AND TIE THEM UP.
TO BE DONE?

5 Team Problem Solving: The Zin Obelisk

Purpose:

I. To experience and examine the sharing of information in team problem solving.

II. To study leadership, cooperation, and conflict issues in team problem solving.

Group Size

A team of five to eight participants.

Time

Approximately fifty-five minutes, including a maximum of twenty-five minutes for completing the activity and between thirty minutes and one hour for the process review.

Materials

I. A copy of the Zin Obelisk Group Instruction Sheet for each participant.

II. A set of Zin Obelisk Information Cards for the group (thirty-three cards per set).

III. A large newsprint pad and felt-tipped markers, or a chalkboard and chalk.

IV. Blank paper and a pencil for each participant.

V. A copy of the Zin Obelisk Review Sheet for the facilitator.

Physical Arrangement

A quiet room in which members of the group are seated in a circle.

The authors acknowledge the contribution of Mike Woodcock, co-author of the original version of this activity.

Method

I.   The leader distributes to each team member a copy of the Zin Obelisk Group Instruction Sheet, paper, and a pencil.

II. After the members have had time to read the instruction sheet, the leader distributes a set of Zin Obelisk Information Cards randomly among the team members. The team begins the task.

III. The team completes the task, or is interrupted by the leader after twenty-five minutes.

IV. The leader reviews the experience with the team, posting a large copy of the Zin Obelisk Review Sheet, and, if necessary, the Answer and Rationale information.

Variations

I.   Any number of groups may be directed simultaneously. A set of Zin Obelisk Information Cards should be provided for each group.

II. Participants may complete the Review Sheets individually before the group process takes place.

III. Extra irrelevant information may be introduced to complicate the task.

ZIN OBELISK INFORMATION CARDS

Make a set of thirty-three cards by typing each of the following sentences on a 3 " x 5 " card. A set should be distributed randomly among the members of the group.

1. The basic measurement of time in Atlantis is a day.
2. An Atlantian day is divided into schlibs and ponks.
3. The length of the zin is 50 feet.
4. The height of the zin is 100 feet.
5. The width of the zin is 10 feet.
6. The zin is built of stone blocks.
7. Each block is 1 cubic foot.
8. Day 1 in the Atlantian week is called Aquaday.
9. Day 2 in the Atlantian week is called Neptiminus.
10. Day 3 in the Atlantian week is called Sharkday.
11. Day 4 in the Atlantian week is called Mermaidday.
12. Day 5 in the Atlantian week is called Daydoldrum.
13. There are five days in an Atlantian week.
14. The working day has 9 schlibs.
15. Each worker takes rest periods during the working day totaling 16 ponks.
16. There are 8 ponks in a schlib.
17. Workers each lay 150 blocks per schlib.
18. At any time when work is taking place there is a gang of 9 people on site.
19. One member of each gang has religious duties and does not lay blocks.
20. No works takes place on Daydoldrum.
21. What is a cubitt?
22. A cubitt is a cube, all sides of which measure 1 megalithic yard.
23. There are 3½ feet in a megalithic yard.
24. Does work take place on Sunday?
25. What is a zin?
26. Which way up does the zin stand?
27. The zin is made up of green blocks.
28. Green has special religious significance on Mermaidday.
29. Each gang includes two women.

30. Work starts at daybreak on Aquaday.
31. Only one gang is working on the construction of the zin.
32. There are eight gold scales in a gold fin.
33. Each block costs 2 gold fins.

ANSWER AND RATIONALE

The answer is *Neptiminus.*

Rationale

1. The dimensions of the zin indicate that it contains 50,000 cubic feet of stone blocks.
2. The blocks are 1 cubic foot each, therefore, 50,000 blocks are required.
3. Each worker works 7 schlibs in a day (2 schlibs are devoted to rest).
4. Each worker lays 150 blocks per schlib, therefore each worker lays 1050 blocks per day.
5. There are 8 workers per day, therefore 8,400 blocks are laid per working day.
6. The 50,000th block, therefore, is laid on the sixth working day.
7. Since work does not take place on Daydoldrum, the sixth working day is Neptiminus.

ZIN OBELISK GROUP INSTRUCTION SHEET

In the ancient city of Atlantis, a solid, rectangular obelisk, called a zin, was built in honor of the goddess Tina. The structure took less than two weeks to complete.

The task of your team is to determine on which day of the week the obelisk was completed. You have twenty-five minutes for this task. Do *not* choose a formal leader.

You will be given cards containing information related to the task. You may share this information orally, but you may not show your cards to other participants.

ZIN OBELISK REVIEW SHEET

1. What behavior helped the group accomplish the task?

2. What behavior hindered the group in completing the task?

3. How did leadership emerge in the team?

4. Who participated most?

5. Who participated least?

6. What feelings did you experience as the task progressed?

7. What suggestions would you make to improve team performance?

⑥ Stages of Team Development

Purpose

I. To provide a framework for a team to evaluate its current stage of development.

II. To choose and set priorities for activities to be undertaken to enhance a team's development.

Time

At least forty-five minutes.

Materials

I. A copy of the Stages of Team Development section (see pages 9-11) of this book, a copy of the Team-Development Wheel, and a pencil for each participant.

II. A large newsprint pad and felt-tipped markers, or a chalkboard and chalk.

Method

I. The leader distributes copies of both the Stages of Team Development section and the Team-Development Wheel to each team member and gives the following instructions:

1. Read the Stages of Team Development section.

2. Look at the Team-Development Wheel diagram and make a mark on the circumference to indicate the current stage of team development. Do not discuss your views at this stage.

II. The leader draws a Team-Development Wheel on the newsprint pad and records the members' evaluation scores on the wheel as they are reported.

III. The results are discussed for further development. At this stage, it will be helpful for each team member to explain and clarify his views on the team's stage of development. If possible, specific examples of behaviors that relate to a particular stage of development should be examined.

IV. Through discussion, and with the help of the leader, the team reaches a consensual assessment of its status. From this basis, the members consider a sequence of activities which will help to develop the team's maturity.

TEAM-DEVELOPMENT WHEEL

Instructions: Place a mark on the circumference of the wheel to represent the present status of your team.

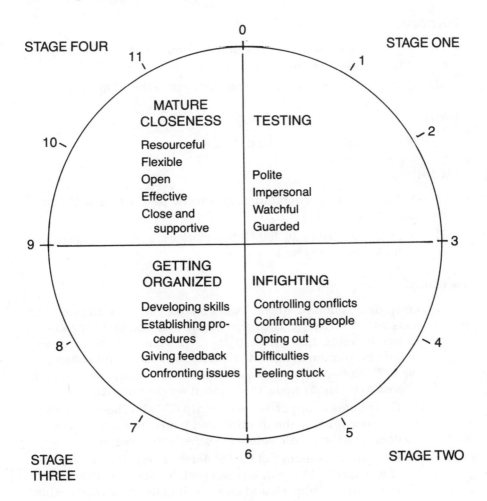

7 Defining Leadership Style: A Sharing Activity

Purpose

I. To help the team and team manager understand and clarify the manager's leadership style.

II. To help the team members give feedback to the team leader.

Time

Between one and two hours.

Materials

I. A copy of the Leadership Style Profile and a pencil for each participant.

II. A large newsprint pad, felt-tipped markers, and masking tape, or a chalkboard and chalk.

Method

I. Open discussion of a team leader's style can be a difficult and sensitive activity for both the leader and the team members. Before entering into this activity, it is essential that all team members voluntarily agree to participate. Participants often prefer to keep their evaluations of the leader anonymous. If they choose to be anonymous, the leader does the following:

    1. Distributes a copy of the Leadership Style Profile to each team member prior to the meeting and instructs each member to complete the profile before the scheduled meeting.

    2. Prepares a large copy of the Leadership Style Profile on pages of newsprint. This will be used both for showing the leader's evaluation of himself and for recording the members' evaluation scores. The individual responses can be tallied above each number on the seven-point scale. Individual requests for more of a particular characteristic can be tallied on the margin next to the item as shown here.

The authors gratefully acknowledge the contribution of Celia Palfreyman in preparing this activity and activities 8, 9, and 38.

More of	Characteristic	Evaluation Scale	Characteristic
Ⅳ⅃	Delegates in order to develop people	1 2 3 4 5 6 7	Delegates only to get tasks performed

II. The team meets and submits the completed Leadership Style Profiles to the leader, who records the members' responses on the large profile along with his own self-evaluation.

III. The group discusses each item of the Leadership Style Profile in order to clarify the responses and their causes. It is helpful to give specific examples of the leader's behaviors if the participants are willing to be this open.

IV. The leader tallies on the large copy of the Leadership Style Profile the characteristics the members want more of from the leader. The team identifies particular items that represent leadership characteristics they would like changed, and the leader reviews his self-rating.

V. The "more of" statements are discussed until points of agreement are noted, and the leader may wish to record an action statement for the team, beginning with:

In the future, I will do more of . . .

LEADERSHIP STYLE PROFILE

Name_____

Instructions: Please give your candid opinion of the leader of this team by rating the leader's characteristics on the seven-point scales shown below. Circle the appropriate number on each scale to represent your evaluation. If you would like the leader to display more of a particular characteristic, circle the description of that characteristic.

Delegates in order to develop people	1 2 3 4 5 6 7	Delegates only to get tasks performed
Spends time collecting ideas and contributions	1 2 3 4 5 6 7	Spends most time selling ideas and persuading people
Involves members in all decisions	1 2 3 4 5 6 7	Involves members in minor decisions
Values and uses the full contribution of all team members	1 2 3 4 5 6 7	Has not fully explored team members' contributions
Gains support through well considered and respected values	1 2 3 4 5 6 7	Gains support from the team by position, status, and influence
Allows autonomy within the team	1 2 3 4 5 6 7	Allows discussions but then makes the major decisions
Has a consistent, well-grounded approach	1 2 3 4 5 6 7	Is swayed by argument and situational problems
Has clearly analyzed his role and negotiated it with the group	1 2 3 4 5 6 7	Tends to keep his problems private and finds it difficult to be open

Recognizes his accountability for team work but leaves responsibility within the team	1	2	3	4	5	6	7	Believes that the work of the team is his sole responsibility
Encourages creativity	1	2	3	4	5	6	7	Tends to cut off members' creative contributions
Is prepared to take risks	1	2	3	4	5	6	7	Prefers to play safe at work
Encourages feedback in order to adapt his operating style	1	2	3	4	5	6	7	Has difficulty in asking for and accepting feedback
Values learning and looks for learning opportunities	1	2	3	4	5	6	7	Usually operates in the same way without reviewing the lessons learned
Creates psychological distance from the team	1	2	3	4	5	6	7	Is part of the team
Is consistent in behavior towards team members	1	2	3	4	5	6	7	Behavior toward team is variable and difficult to predict

⑧ The Best Leaders I Have Known

Purpose

To help team members define positive leadership characteristics and share these definitions with the team leader.

Time

One hour.

Materials

I. One large copy of the Sample Descriptions of Leadership Characteristics sheet for display.

II. A large newsprint pad, felt-tipped markers, and masking tape, or a chalkboard and chalk.

III. Blank paper and pencil for each participant.

Method

I. The leader distributes paper and pencils to the team members with the following instructions:
   1. Identify a good leader you have worked for or read about.
   2. List at least six outstanding personal characteristics that this leader appeared to possess.

II. The leader posts the Sample Descriptions of Leadership Characteristics, warning the members not to copy the descriptions but to use them only as examples of the way in which such characteristics might be described.

III. Team members complete their lists. (Ten minutes.)

IV. The facilitator charts each member's list and leads the team in a discussion focused on:
   1. Clarifying the lists of descriptions.
   2. Finding common characteristics in the lists.
   3. Ranking the top three characteristics the team would like to see developed in the behavior of team members.
   4. Identifying actions the team could take to help reinforce or develop these characteristics.

SAMPLE DESCRIPTIONS OF LEADERSHIP CHARACTERISTICS

The effective leader:

1. Tries to see the merit in your ideas even if they conflict with his own.
2. Has consistently high expectations of subordinates.
3. Tries to encourage people to reach out in new directions.
4. Takes your mistakes in stride as long as you can learn from them.
5. Expects superior performance and gives credit when it is achieved.
6. Tries to help his people understand overall organizational objectives.
7. Is easy to talk to even when under pressure.
8. Tries to give people the information they want.
9. Freely gives positive, helping feedback.
10. etc.

⑨ Who Performs the Leadership Functions?

Purpose

I. To help a team understand how leadership functions are currently carried out in the team.

II. To determine the best ways of carrying out leadership functions in the future.

Time

A maximum of two hours. It may be worthwhile to repeat this activity periodically as the team develops maturity and flexibility of operation.

Materials

I. A copy of the Leadership Functions Check Sheet and a pencil for each participant.

II. A large newsprint pad and felt-tipped markers, or a chalkboard and chalk.

Method

I. This project should be undertaken only with the voluntary agreement of all concerned. A copy of the Leadership Functions Check Sheet is circulated to participants a few days before the planned session with a covering note asking whether people have any reservations. Once voluntary participation has been affirmed, the project can go ahead.

II. Each team member, including the team manager, should complete the check sheet before the team meeting or at the beginning of the meeting.

III. The leader charts each item on the check sheet separately and tallies the individual responses. If any member has reservations about openly sharing his personal views, all the completed check sheets can be submitted anonymously.

IV. The team discusses each item, concentrating on areas that seem to require some change in methods of work or behavior. When the discussion is completed, the items suggested for change are listed for the whole team to review until consensus is reached.

LEADERSHIP FUNCTIONS CHECK SHEET

Instructions: The following are kinds of leadership behavior that usually are engaged in by someone in a group. Read each item carefully and mark a check [✔] under the phrase that most accurately describes whoever performs that function in your team.

	No One	Formal Leader	Group Members (give names if possible)
1. Who usually brings together individual contributions?			
2. Who ensures that the team makes decisions?			
3. Who begins our meetings or starts our work?			
4. Who keeps a check on whether objectives are set?			
5. Who ensures that we follow an effective method of working together?			
6. Who puts energy into the team to start us off or help us when we seem stuck?			
7. Who watches over our operation and picks us up if we omit stages of working?			
8. Who finds and brings in external information to help our work stay relevant?			

9. Who represents us as a team with other groups or teams?

10. Who summarizes and clarifies after our discussions?

11. Who encourages contributions from team members?

12. Who supports other members in difficult situations?

10 Negotiating the Team Manager's Role

Purpose

I. To clarify the team manager's expectations of the team and the team members' expectations of their manager.

II. To identify significant differences in these expectations.

Time

A minimum of two hours.

Materials

I. A large newsprint pad, felt-tipped markers, and masking tape, or a chalkboard and chalk.

II. Blank paper and a pencil for each participant.

Method

I. It is important that the team members undertake the activity voluntarily and review the results together.

II. The leader distributes paper and pencils and asks the team members to complete the following statements:
1. What I expect the team manager of this group to do is:
2. What I expect that the team manager wants me to do as a member of this group is:

III. While the members are completing their statements, the leader completes his own set of statements.
1. My most important contributions to the team are:
2. What I want the team to do is (specific examples should be given when possible):

IV. The leader charts and posts all the items in the following format:

	Team Members' Views	Leader's Views
Leader's Role		
Team's Role		

V. In a group discussion, the team deals with its responses concerning the leader's role:

1. After common points are agreed on, they are listed on a new sheet.

2. The remaining points are discussed one by one. When difficulties occur, the procedure can be reversed, i.e., the team manager speaks as a team member and a team member speaks as the team manager. When agreement is reached, the points are added to the chart. If significant differences of opinion still remain, the team does the following:

   • Define the remaining points of difference as clearly as possible and chart them.

   • For each charted point of significant difference, each member should complete the following sentence.

     The following could be done to reduce the difference:

   • The members disclose their suggestions, and the group discusses the feasibility of the suggestions and reaches consensus on as many as possible.

VI. In a similar way, the responses concerning the role of the team members are charted and discussed.

VII. The team members now can use the two charts as checklists to review their roles and see how effective they are. Tasks that previously have been successful and unsuccessful can be reviewed against the checklists.

Notes

I. The value of this activity depends on the open discussion of roles and expectations.

II. This type of discussion may need to be held regularly—perhaps every three months—with a developing team.

11 Team Skills Audit

Purpose

I.   To identify the social and technical skills required by the team.

II. To evaluate the team's present skills.

III. To select the skill areas most in need of development.

Time

Approximately two hours.

Materials

I.   A copy each of the Team Skills Audit Sheets, Part 1 and Part 2, and a pencil for each participant.

II. A large newsprint pad, felt-tipped markers, and masking tape, or a chalkboard and chalk.

Method

I.   This activity may highlight some issues that are sensitive to the whole team or to individuals within it. Therefore, the voluntary agreement of the entire team must be obtained prior to the beginning of the activity.

II. The leader distributes to each member a copy of Part 1 of the Team Skills Audit Sheet and a pencil.

III. The leader asks the members to read the instructions and complete the audit sheets. While they are working, the leader prepares a large copy of both audit sheets (Parts 1 and 2) on the newsprint pad and posts it.

IV. Using the large audit sheet for Part 1, the leader tallies the priority scores given to each statement by the individual members. The resulting total is entered next to each statement on the large audit sheet in the "Personal Score" column.

V.   The team assigns a group priority number to each of the statements by discussing any significant differences that members have concerning the tallied results of the personal scores. When agreement is reached on the group scores, they are entered in the "Group Score" column on the posted audit sheet.

VI.   After the team has seen the group score rankings, the leader distributes to each member a copy of Part 2 of the Team Skills Audit Sheet and directs the members to read the instructions and complete the sheet.

VII.   The leader repeats the procedure previously used for posting and tallying personal scores and records the resulting total in the "Personal Rating" column of the posted audit sheet for Part 2.

VIII.   The team discusses the personal ratings in order to reach consensus on the group's evaluation of each skill area. These are charted by the leader.

IX.   When the members can see the rankings, the top five priority skills that have a ranking of 2 or 3 are highlighted. These skill areas are the most important for the team to work on and, if necessary, to seek help in developing.

TEAM SKILLS AUDIT SHEET, PART 1

Instructions: Evaluate the following statements in relation to your team and assign a priority to each, using the key shown below. Add any skills that you require, but which are missing from the list, and assign priority numbers to each of them. Enter the scores in the column headed "Personal Score."

KEY

3 = Vital to the success of the team

2 = Important to the success of the team

1 = Useful to the success of the team

0 = Irrelevant to the success of the team

Statements	Personal Score	Group Score
1. Skillful and positive leadership		
2. Clear identification of objectives		
3. Creative and innovative ideas		
4. Realistic planning		
5. Ability to get things done		
6. Good conceptual and theoretical ability		
7. Effective trouble shooting		
8. Persuasive communication		
9. Imaginative design skills		
10. Technical expertise		
11. Financial expertise		
12. Production expertise		
13. Personnel expertise		
14. Marketing expertise		
15. etc.		
16.		
17.		

TEAM SKILLS AUDIT SHEET, PART 2

Instructions: Transfer the top fifteen statements from Part 1 to this sheet, listing them in rank order. Evaluate each statement in relation to your team, using the rating key shown below. Enter the scores in the column headed "Personal Rating."

KEY

1 = The team has adequate skills in this area.

2 = There is a need to improve skills in this area.

3 = We do not have any skills and need to develop them.

Top 15 Skills	Personal Rating	Group Rating
1.		
2.		
3.		
4.		
5.		
6.		
7.		
8.		
9.		
10.		
11.		
12.		
13.		
14.		
15.		

12 Selecting a New Team Member

Purpose

To help a team develop a consensual approach to selecting a new member of the team.

Time

Approximately one and one-half hours.

Materials

A large newsprint pad, felt-tipped markers, and masking tape, or a chalkboard and chalk.

Method

I. The leader asks the team members to work individually on defining their views concerning:

1. The primary purpose of the job for which a new team member is being recruited. (It may be helpful to complete the sentence, "The primary purpose of this job is to . . . .")
2. The team members with whom the new member will have to work, and for what reason.
3. The main skills that are needed for the job. (It may be helpful to split these into technical and personal skills.)
4. The best kind of person for the job. (It may be helpful to write a short paragraph that begins, "The kind of person I would most like to see in the job would . . . .")

II. The members discuss, define, and chart the following:

1. The members' views under headings 1, 2, 3, and 4.
2. Similar factors under each heading.
3. The major elements of dissimilarity between members' lists.

III. The team works through the dissimilarities between their views, exploring *why* there are differences and negotiating the closest approximation of consensus they can reach.

IV. The leader arranges to have the team's four consensual definitions typed and distributed to each member of the team who sees potential recruits. A prospective member should be seen by as many members of the team as possible before the final selection is made.

13 Use Us, We're the Best

Purpose

I. To critically review the skills, capabilities, and potential of a team.

II. To evaluate the marketability of a team.

Time

Two hours.

Materials

I. A large newsprint pad and felt-tipped markers, or a chalkboard and chalk.

II. Blank paper and a pencil for each participant.

Method

I. The leader distributes paper and pencils to the members. He tells the team to imagine that it is currently acting as an internal consulting unit in a very large organization. Times are very hard commercially. Yesterday, the consulting unit's manager was called in to see his boss, who said: "I'm sorry to have to say this, but we have reached a critical point, and it is questionable whether this company can survive. As you know, we are a decent outfit and have never fired people unless absolutely necessary. The way things are, I see two alternatives for your department. First, we can close it down. Second, you can market the team's services outside this company in order to cover more than 50 percent of your budget. I know that the market is tough and the competition strong, but I think you can do it. You can hire in some additional skills if you want to, provided you cover the costs. You have six months to plan and prepare for the launch."

II. The leader helps the group perform the following tasks, while reminding the members to keep in mind the background information:

1. Analyze the skills and capabilities you have in the team that would be useful to other organizations.

2. Identify any shortcomings of your team and any additional skills you would like to hire in.

3. Decide, considering the six months of intensive effort allowed for preparation, what you would do to enhance the skills you already have.

4. Prepare a brochure, advertising your new team to potential customers.

5. Review what you have learned from this activity, in particular, where you need to enhance your skills or develop the skills you already have. List and retain the major conclusions.

He provides the team with blank newsprint and felt-tipped markers and tells the members that they will have ninety minutes in which to complete their task.

III. At the end of the allotted time, the leader stops the activity and assists the team members in reporting out their activities and what they discovered during the activity.

14 Test Your Commitment

Purpose

To help a team identify factors that increase or decrease the level of members' commitment (positive identification with the team and its objectives).

Time

One hour.

Materials

I. A copy of the Commitment Chart and a pencil for each participant.

II. A large newsprint pad, felt-tipped markers, and masking tape, or a chalkboard and chalk.

Method

I. The leader distributes to each participant a copy of the Commitment Chart and a pencil.

II. The team members are directed to read the instructions and complete their charts.

III. The members' charts can be shared either by posting them for all to see, or the leader can record the results on a large sheet of newsprint and post this master chart.

IV. With the leader's help, the members brainstorm ideas for increasing positive factors affecting members' commitment and for decreasing negative factors.

COMMITMENT CHART

Instructions: This Commitment Chart lists a number of factors that may affect a member's positive or negative feelings of commitment toward the team and its work. These may be regarded as forces working for or against a satisfactory level of commitment.

1. Review the commitment statements listed below and mark any items that you think are relevant for you.
2. At the end of the list, write (and number) any additional factors that you feel are affecting your level of commitment in your team.
3. Enter in the "Forces Affecting The Commitment of the Team" columns the numbers of the factors you have identified as relevant. Forces identified as contributing to high commitment should be entered on the right side of the center line, and those contributing to a lack of commitment should be entered on the left.

COMMITMENT STATEMENTS

1. Your identification with the whole team
2. Your belief in the team's aims
3. The ability of the team to produce in accordance with these aims
4. The team's support for individuals
5. The time and energy spent in developing the team
6. Clarity about what the team is trying to achieve
7. Feedback and approval among team members
8. Feedback and approval from the rest of the organization
9. Identification of worthwhile role in the wider organization

Add any other factors relevant to your team:

FORCES AFFECTING THE COMMITMENT OF THE TEAM

Low Commitment	High Commitment

15 Increasing Team Commitment: An Adventure Project

Purpose

I.   To acquaint and involve team members with one another in more depth.

II. To develop informal ties between team members.

III. To increase the members' feelings of commitment to the team.

Method

I.   The leader explains that, based on the principle that involvement in a fairly vigorous and outdoor team project is a rapid and effective way to develop team cooperation and morale, the team will undertake a two-day activity that involves physical activity, some deprivation, enjoyment, and success. The team is asked to undertake an activity that will require unusual exertion. In many areas, outdoor pursuit centers or local associations will be able to suggest suitable projects and provide leadership.

II. The team discusses the opportunities and chooses something similar to the following activities:

1. Sailing a boat on a two-day journey.
2. Rock climbing or extended mountain walking.
3. Canoeing.
4. Solving military-style outdoor problems.
5. Raising funds for a community project.

III. After a project has been chosen, the team establishes project goals. An example of a goal statement might be: "The goal of this team project is to build a raft from planks, oil drums, and rope and to use the completed raft to ferry all team members across the lake (or river) from point A to point B."

Notes

I.   It is important that the project leader have highly developed skills in the kind of activity undertaken. He can be assisted by a team representative in making arrangements and coordinating the activity.

II. There are potential dangers in a physical activity if the participants do not have the necessary physical health and conditioning. Team members should be made fully aware of the nature of the activity and their participation should be voluntary.

16 Team Counseling

Purpose

I. To allow the team to explore an individual member's feelings about his relationships with the team and give counsel on overcoming any difficulties.

II. To mobilize the support and skills of the team in helping individuals develop their relationships within the group.

Time

A minimum of two hours.

Materials

A large newsprint pad and felt-tipped markers, or a chalkboard and chalk.

Physical Arrangement

One room for the team and an adjoining room suitable for interviews.

Method

I. Positive counseling can be of great value to individuals, but if it is not done carefully and skillfully, it also can be damaging. Before starting the activity, the leader should suggest that the team members read Activity 1, "Giving Feedback." The presence of an experienced advisor may be an advantage for teams that have not experienced any formal team development.

II. The team decides which individual(s) would benefit by receiving counseling and feedback from the rest of the members. It is vital that the person being counseled should wish to receive feedback from the rest of the team and should openly accept that some of the feedback might be of a personal nature or cause some initial discomfort. No team member should be pressured into being counseled.

III. When a volunteer has been identified, he should be directed to a separate room, and another team member should be selected to interview the person to be counseled. (This selection should *not* be made in the presence of the person who is to receive counsel.) Two important criteria in working this selection are:

1. The interviewer selected should wish to take responsibility for working with the individual to be counseled.

2. The interviewer should have confidence in his ability to work with the person to be counseled on issues that may be sensitive.

IV. The team should work with the interviewer to prepare for the interviews. (This should not be done with the interviewee present.)

The leader explains the purpose of the interview. "To collect data on the individual's feelings about his relationships with the team, and, in particular, any negative feelings or difficulties."

The role of other team members should be to help the interviewer identify a list of questions to be covered in the interview, and also to suggest how best the interviewer should conduct the interview session. Examples of relevant questions are:

1. What specific help might the team give the individual in doing his job.

2. What, if any, specific incidents that occurred in the last few months were positive and helpful to you? Were negative for you?

3. Are there any team members with whom you would like to improve your relationships? Which ones? How?

V. The interviewer should then join the interviewee in the separate room to conduct the interview privately, without the rest of the team present.

VI. After the interview, the interviewer should structure the findings, and then spend up to a half-hour informing the rest of the team of the results of the interview.

VII. The team should then prepare as a whole to counsel the individual who was interviewed. They should focus on:

- How we feel you see us as a team.

- How we feel about you as a team member.

- The actions we can take in the future to support and help you overcome any difficulties you may experience as a member of the team.

In giving the feedback, it is usually best for the interviewer to take the initial lead in the feedback session.

VIII. The person to be counseled should then be asked to rejoin the rest of the team, and the counseling session begins. A useful structure for this session could be:

1. The team gives the person to be counseled his initial feedback.

2. Time is allowed for clarification, suggestions, and identification of significant issues by the interviewee.

3. The team and the individual work through issues that they have identified as being significant.

   The emphasis in this step should be on giving clear, helpful feedback, with a focus on "what we can all do to help a valued member of the team." This part of the session can last at least one hour.

IX. At the end of the feedback, the whole team should review the exercise, summarize the main points that emerged, and, when relevant, identify points for future actions. (Up to one-half hour.)

17 The Commitment Problem

Purpose

To examine individual and team motivation and commitment by analyzing the role play of a specific managerial problem.

Time

One hour or longer.

Materials

I.   One copy of the John Rudd Problem Briefing Sheet and a pencil for each participant.

II. A large newsprint pad and felt-tipped markers, or a chalkboard and chalk.

Physical Arrangement

A quiet room for the group meeting and a small room in which the role player can study his role.

Method

I.   The leader distributes to each participant a copy of the John Rudd Problem Briefing Sheet and a pencil and directs the members to read the sheet.

II. The leader helps the team discuss the problem for twenty minutes.

III. The leader asks for a volunteer to role play John Rudd and directs the volunteer to leave the room and prepare for the role by studying the briefing sheet. (If a woman plays the part, then the role should have an appropriate female name, such as Joan Rudd.)

IV. The team discusses the situation and what Roger Smith should do. The leader asks for a volunteer to role play Roger Smith (or Rita Smith). (Fifteen minutes.)

V.   The person who is role playing John Rudd is called back to the room to meet with the person who is role playing Smith. While the other group members silently observe, the two players attempt to work through the problem. (Ten minutes.)

VI.   With the help of the observers' comments, the team reviews the role play for at least twenty minutes.

VII. At the end of the session, one person summarizes the discussion and asks, "What have we learned about commitment in teams?"

THE JOHN RUDD PROBLEM BRIEFING SHEET

John Rudd is forty-one years old and works as a work-study advisor for an engineering company with two thousand employees. He reports to Roger Smith, work-study manager for the company. There are three other advisors on the same level as John Rudd.

The company has been going through a major reorganization because its basic product line has become outdated by the invention of new plastic materials. Several small production units have been closed and the company is reorganizing its factory in Boston to handle the newly developed materials. Overall profitability has been poor in recent years. The top-management group has been forced to take drastic action to try to return the company to profitability.

For the last four months, John Rudd has been assigned to the Boston factory to work on a project basis. His task is "to identify operational and training requirements and ensure that adequate systems and training are planned and conducted." His supervisor, Roger (or Rita) Smith, is based at the company's administrative offices, which are thirty-five miles away. Smith visits Rudd for about half a day every two weeks.

Smith wants to use a team approach within the department and has organized departmental team meetings and worked through several problem-solving exercises. However, Rudd seems resistant to being fully involved. He spends time sitting with a glum expression on his face, and he avoids confronting other team members. When his performance is brought into question, it is typical for him to withdraw, appear hurt and look, as one team member put it, "like a dog forced to eat cabbage." On other occasions, Rudd's behavior is much more positive and open; he offers suggestions and spends time and energy following through on them.

It is apparent that Smith has backed off from dealing with Rudd. Smith has been intimidated by the threat of withdrawal, and knows that it would be difficult to replace a man of Rudd's experience. However, the financial and technical problems in the company require that Smith make a strong contribution to the effectiveness of the Boston factory.

The problem is brought to a head one day when the manager of the Boston factory, James Tait, telephones Smith to complain about John Rudd. Tait says, "Frankly, I'm worried about Rudd's performance. Things frequently are put off and, quite often, I do not get the reports and documents as requested. Although he gets on quite well with the supervisors and operators, he doesn't do so well with me. He seems pessimistic and waits to be asked before acting. There is another matter, quite personal—Rudd has been drinking rather a lot recently. Almost every day, he goes off with some supervisors for a few drinks at lunch time and after work as well. I'm worried. You know how important Boston is to us—I need a good work-study service."

Smith thanked James Tait for the call, and then sat back, thinking, "Well it has come to a head. What needs to be done?"

18 Team-Climate Questionnaire

Purpose

To help a team examine its working climate and prepare an action plan for improving it.

Time

A minimum of forty-five minutes. Groups often find it valuable to recheck the data by administering the questionnaire on later occasions.

Materials

I.   A copy of the Team-Climate Questionnaire and a pencil for each participant.

II. A large newsprint pad and felt-tipped markers, or a chalkboard and chalk.

III. Blank paper and pencil for each participant.

Physical Arrangement

A quiet room, free from interruptions.

Method

I.   The leader prepares a summary chart on the large newsprint pad. (This will be used for summarizing results of the completed questionnaires.)

II. The leader distributes to each team member a copy of the Team-Climate Questionnaire and a pencil.

III. Participants are asked to read the instructions and complete the questionnaire in five minutes.

IV. After the questionnaire has been completed, the leader asks whether the participants want to report their individual scores orally or write them on paper and turn them in anonymously.

V.   The leader collects the scores and posts them on his summary chart, showing the range of scores and the mean score for each item.

VI. The leader helps the team examine and discuss the following:

  1. The mean scores for each item and the range of scores.

2. Whether the team would develop better if its behavior moved more to the left or right side of the scale on each item.

3. The specific team behaviors that relate to each of the items.

4. The overall climate of the group and ideas for improving it.

VII. The team may decide on an action plan at this time. If it does, this should be recorded.

VIII. After the group has worked together on several more occasions, this activity should be repeated and the scores compared with the earlier survey.

TEAM-CLIMATE QUESTIONNAIRE

Instructions: Please give your candid opinions of this team by rating its characteristics on the seven-point scales shown below. Circle the appropriate number on each scale to represent your evaluation.

Openness. Are individuals open in their transactions with others? Are there hidden agendas? Are some topics taboo for discussion within the group? Can team members express their feelings about others openly without offense?

| Individuals are very open | 1 | 2 | 3 | 4 | 5 | 6 | 7 | Individuals are very guarded |

Conformity. Does the group have rules, procedures, policies, and traditions that are preventing it from working effectively? Are the ideas of senior members considered as law? Can individuals freely express unusual or unpopular views?

| Rigid conformity to an inappropriate pattern | 1 | 2 | 3 | 4 | 5 | 6 | 7 | Open group with a flexible pattern |

Support. Do team members pull for one another? What happens when an individual makes a mistake? Do members who are strong expend energy in helping members who are less experienced or less capable?

| High level support for individuals | 1 | 2 | 3 | 4 | 5 | 6 | 7 | Little help for individuals |

Confronting Difficulties. Are diffiicult or uncomortable issues openly worked through? Are conflicts confronted or swept under the carpet? Can team members openly disagree with the team manager? Does the team devote much energy to thoroughly working through difficulties?

| Difficult issues are avoided | 1 | 2 | 3 | 4 | 5 | 6 | 7 | Problems are attacked openly and directly |

Risk Taking. Do individuals feel that they can try new things, risk failure, and still get support? Does the team positively encourage people to extend themselves?

Risk taking in work not encouraged	1	2	3	4	5	6	7	Experimentation and personal exploration are the norm

Shared Values. Have team members worked through their own values with others? Is time spent on considering the cause (Why?) as well as the effect (What?)? Is there a fundamental set of values shared by team members?

No basis of common values	1	2	3	4	5	6	7	Large area of common ground.

Energy. Do team members put sufficient energy into working on relationships with others? Does team membership act as a stimulus and energizer to individuals?

High level of positive energy	1	2	3	4	5	6	7	Little energy directed toward team

19 From Me to You, From You to Me

Purpose

I. To provide team members with a structured and practical means of giving feedback to one another.

II. To help team members work through problems in personal and work relationships.

Time

Between one and two hours will be needed for the initial meeting. Several meetings may be required to work through all issues suggested by team members.

Materials

I. Sufficient copies of the From Me to You, From You to Me Message Sheets for each team member to send to every other member of the team.

II. A large newsprint pad and felt-tipped markers, or a chalkboard and chalk.

III. Blank paper and a pencil for each participant.

IV. Masking tape (optional).

Method

I. The leader distributes a Message Sheet, paper, and a pencil to each participant. The leader says that each member is to fill out a message sheet for every other member of the team.

II. Participants are asked to stand and deliver the messages by laying them on the recipient's empty chair.

III. Each person reads and silently reacts to the messages he has received.

IV. The team leader asks team members to seek maximum clarity and understanding of the messages by openly discussing them.

This activity was developed from an idea by Roger Harrison of Development Research Associates.

Members are encouraged to make specific feedback statements, with examples of behavior if necessary.

V.   After the discussion, the members enter into negotiations directed at getting commitments to specific future actions. Statements such as "In the future I will do . . . ." may be helpful.

VI. Statements of agreed actions can be written and displayed for confirmation.

Variations

I.   If the team feels secure about doing it, each member fills in a message sheet directed *only* to those persons with whom he has problems.

II. Team members decide with which persons they would most like to explore their messages and negotiate to set up one-to-one meetings.

III. Each set of messages is displayed for the whole team to see and review.

FROM ME TO YOU, FROM YOU TO ME MESSAGE SHEET

MESSAGES FROM_____TO_____

It would be more comfortable and beneficial for me if you would . . .

1. Do the following things *more* or *better:*

2. Do the following things *less,* or *stop doing them:*

3. Continue doing the following things:

4. Start doing these additional things:

20 Cave Rescue

Purpose

I. To examine the impact of individual values and attitudes on group decision making.

II. To study problem-solving procedures in groups.

III. To practice consensus-seeking behavior.

Group Size

Any number of groups, comprising four to seven participants, may be directed simultaneously.

Materials

I. A copy each of the Cave Rescue Briefing Sheet, the Cave Rescue Biographical Sheet, the Cave Rescue Review Sheet, and a pencil for each participant.

II. A Cave Rescue Ranking Sheet for each group.

III. A large newsprint pad and felt-tipped markers, or a chalkboard and chalk.

Physical Arrangement

A room large enough to accommodate a circle of chairs for each group with the groups sufficiently separated to allow privacy.

Method

I. The leader briefly explains the goals of the activity.

II. The leader divides the participants into equally-sized groups of four to seven members. He asks that each group seat its members in a circle and separate the circles enough to allow privacy for each group.

The authors acknowledge the contribution of Mike Woodcock, co-author of the original version of this activity.

III. A Cave Rescue Briefing Sheet, a Cave Rescue Biographical Sheet, and a pencil are distributed to each of the participants. They are allowed five minutes to read the materials and assimilate the data.

IV. After five minutes, the leader directs each group to discuss the Ranking Sheet within forty-five minutes. A Cave Rescue Ranking Sheet is given to each group.

V. When the time is up, the leader collects the ranking sheets and distributes the Cave Rescue Review Sheet to all participants.

VI. The participants complete the review sheets and share their responses with one another.

VII. The leader helps the entire group to discuss the experience, using the participants' reactions to the questions on the Cave Rescue Review Sheet.

Notes and Variations

I. Additional characters can be created.

II. Some members may be designated to observe the group process and then use their observations to help the group discussion of the experience.

III. Because some group members may not wish to take part in the activity for ethical reasons, participation should be voluntary.

CAVE RESCUE BRIEFING SHEET

Your group is asked to take the role of a Research Management Committee responsible for administering research projects in the behavioral
sciences at State University. You have been called to an emergency
meeting because of a catastrophe in one of the projects for which the
committee is responsible.

The project, which is studying human behavior in confined spaces,
is conducting an experiment in a remote part of the country. The experiment involves six volunteers living underground in a cave system for
four days. The group's only outside connection is a radio link to a
research station at the cave entrance. A call for help has been received
from the volunteers—they have been trapped in a cave by falling rocks
and water is rising in the cave.

The only available rescue team reports that rescue will be extremely
difficult and, with the equipment at its disposal, only one person can be
brought out each hour. This makes it likely that the rapidly rising water
will drown some of the volunteers before rescue can be effected.

Through their radio link with the research station, the volunteers
have been made aware of the dangers of their plight. They have communicated that they are unwilling to decide on the sequence by which they
will be rescued. The responsibility for making this decision now rests
with the Research Management Committee; you must decide the order
of rescue.

Life-saving equipment will arrive in fifty minutes at the cave
entrance. Before that time, you must provide the rescue team with
a sequential list—a rank-order sheet—for rescuing the trapped
volunteers.

The only available information has been drawn from the project files
and is reproduced on the Cave Rescue Biographical Sheet. You may use
any criteria you think fit to help you make a decision. A Cave Rescue
Ranking Sheet should be completed by your group and submitted
within fifty minutes.

CAVE RESCUE BIOGRAPHICAL SHEET

Volunteer 1.   Helen: White, Female, American, Age 34.

Helen is married and a homemaker. Her husband is a member of the city council. She had been a promising psychology student before leaving the university to be married. Helen has four children (aged 7 months to 8 years) and lives in a pleasant suburban community near the university. Her hobbies are ice skating and cooking. Helen became involved in the experiment through Owen, with whom she has developed a covert sexual relationship.

Volunteer 2.   Tozo: Oriental, Female, Japanese, Age 19.

Tozo is single, and a sociology student at State University. Her wealthy Japanese parents live in Tokyo, where her father is an industrialist and a national authority on traditional Japanese mime theater. Tozo is outstandingly attractive and has several "upper-crust" boyfriends. She recently was among several women featured in a television documentary on Japanese womanhood.

Volunteer 3.   John: Black, Male, American, Age 41.

John is married, and campus coordinator of Catholic Social Services at State University. He has five children (aged 6 years to 19 years). John worked full time while attending the university and he earned a master's degree in social work. For many years he has been deeply involved in a militant black civil rights group. His hobbies are photography and camping out with his family.

Volunteer 4.   Owen: White, Male, American, Age 27.

Owen is unmarried, and a physical education instructor at University High School. He joined the Army after high school, became an infantry platoon leader in Viet Nam, where he received several distinguished decorations. He was sent home with a serious leg wound from which he has recovered (except for occasional pains). He used his GI Bill benefits to earn a master's degree in physical education. Since returning to civilian life, Owen has been unsettled and his drinking has become a persistent problem. His recreation is modifying and driving stock cars.

Volunteer 5.   Paul: White, Male, English, Age 47.

Paul is divorced, and a medical research scientist at the university hospital. He is recognized as a world authority on the treatment of rabies. Paul is testing a new, experimental low-cost rabies treatment, but much of the research data is still in his working notebooks. His hobbies are classical music and sailing. Paul's ex-wife is happily re-married but in the six years since the divorce, he has experienced some emotional difficulties. He has no children. He was twice convicted of indecent exposure (the last occasion was eleven months ago).

Volunteer 6.   Edward: White, Male, American, Age 59.

Edward is married, and has two grown children who have moved away to large cities and have their own families. He is general manager of a small factory producing rubber belts for machines. The factory employs seventy-one persons. Edward has personally negotiated a large contract for his company and final contract details are awaiting his return to work. This contract, if signed, would mean employment for another eighty-five people. Active socially and politically in the community, Edward is a senior freemason and a member of the city council. His hobby is spelunking (exploring caves) and he intends to write a book about the subject when he retires.

CAVE RESCUE RANKING SHEET

Instructions: Your task is to rank the six trapped individuals in terms of their value by writing each of their names next to a number that indi-cates their order of rescue.

ORDER OF RESCUE	NAME
1	
2	
3	
4	
5	
6	

CAVE RESCUE REVIEW SHEET

1. What were the principal criteria used in ranking the volunteers?

2. How closely did the group's criteria line up with your own?

3. How comfortable did you feel about making this kind of decision?

4. Were there any individuals with whom you strongly disagreed? How do you feel about these individuals now?

5. What behaviors helped the group in arriving at a decision?

6. What behaviors hindered the group in arriving at a decision?

21 Defining the Team's Maintenance and Achievement Activities

Introduction

Teams often run into problems in their work because they are confused about the amount of energy spent on *maintenance* activities—performed to maintain the team's internal workings or procedures—and *achievement* activities—directly related to the attaining of the team's goals over a specific time span. This lack of clarity can lead to wasted energy and low achievement.

Purpose

I.   To enable each team member to classify his work activities and the time allocated to them under the categories of maintenance or achievement.

II. To analyze the whole team's work activities, determine whether they are sufficient, and if not, plan changes.

Time

A minimum of one hour.

Materials

I.   A copy of the Team Activities Chart and a pencil for each participant.

II. A large newsprint pad and felt-tipped markers, or a chalkboard and chalk.

Method

I.   The leader distributes to each participant a copy of the Team Activities Chart and a pencil.

II. Team members are asked to record on the chart their activities over a specific time frame, such as one month.

1.   Members roughly allocate a percentage of the total time they have available for each activity. This can be done from memory or from logging the time as it is spent.

2. Members categorize the activities as achievement or maintenance and record them under the appropriate headings.

III. At the team meeting, each member is asked to share his allocation data with the others, and the leader charts the activity allocation for the whole team.

IV. The leader leads the team in a discussion of the following questions:

1. Is the allocation of activities satisfactory in the light of the team's performance?

2. If changes are needed, what actions should we take in order to bring them about?

TEAM ACTIVITIES CHART

		ALLOCATION	
		---	---
All Major Activities	% of Time	Achievement of Team Goals	Maintenance of Team's Internal Order
		% of Time on Achievement Tasks_____	% of Time on Maintenance Tasks_____

Identifying Team Success

Purpose

I. To examine the past activity of a team.

II. To evaluate and chart the successes and failures of a team.

III. To use the evaluation information in predicting a team's future effectiveness.

Time

A minimum of one and one-half hours.

Materials

I. A roll of white paper nine feet long.

II. Masking tape or some other method of affixing the paper to a wall without damaging the wall.

III. A large newsprint pad and felt-tipped markers, or a chalkboard and chalk.

IV. Blank paper and a pencil for each participant.

Physical Arrangement

A room with sufficient wall space to display the nine-foot chart.

Method

I. Before the meeting, the leader should prepare a Team Success Chart (A), similar to the sample diagram shown, on the nine-foot-long strip of paper. The chart is then affixed horizontally to the wall.

II. The leader explains the Team Success Chart while drawing a smaller version of it (B) on the large newsprint pad. He draws a dotted line (see sample diagram) on Chart B as an example of a trend line.

III. Paper and pencils are distributed to the members. They are instructed to reproduce the chart and draw a trend line representing their own evaluations of the team's success throughout the past year.

IV.   When the individual diagrams are completed, the leader does the following (one hour):

1. Collects the diagrams and charts all the individual trend lines on the smaller chart (B).

2. Makes an estimate of the team mean for each month and draws a line on the Team Success Chart (A) representing the overall team pattern.

3. Leads the members in determining reasons for any sharp shifts in the team's trend line.

4. Writes the reason for a shift near the location of the shift on the Team Success Chart (A).

V.   The team looks ahead at future events,which are plotted in the right-hand section of the Team Success Chart (A). The effectiveness of the team in dealing with these future events is predicted on a month-by-month basis, and a dotted line is drawn to represent the trend line of future success.

SUCCESS CHART

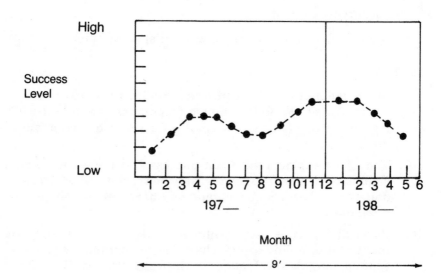

 **New Game**

Purpose

I. To examine the dynamics of a team's performance in producing a tangible result within a short time period.

II. To observe the effect of feedback on team performance.

Time

One and one-half hours.

Materials

I. A copy of the New Game Review Sheet and a pencil for each participant.

II. Ten coins of the same value, one pack of playing cards, and one large bag of chocolates.

III. A large newsprint pad and felt-tipped markers, or a chalkboard and chalk.

Physical Arrangement

One room for the meeting and a smaller room in which the visitors can wait. A table will be needed in the meeting room for display of the game materials.

Background

Arrangements should be made for two persons who are not members of the team to join the group as visitors at Step Two. Brief the two on what will be expected of them and the time involved.

Method

I. Step One

The leader explains to the group that it has forty minutes in which to create a new game for two persons. He instructs them to use only the materials provided, devise the game rules, and prepare to teach the game to two people who will visit the group in forty minutes.

II. Step Two

1. The visitors arrive and are asked to play the new game for ten minutes.
2. Following this, the visitors are asked to comment to the group on the strengths and weaknesses of the new game, then they leave the room. (Approximately fifteen minutes.)

III. Step Three

The leader directs the group to improve the game it has devised, using the comments received, and complete the changes in fifteen minutes.

IV. Step Four

1. The visitors return and play the revised game for ten minutes.
2. The visitors are asked to comment on the game and then they leave the group. (Approximately fifteen minutes.)

V. Step Five

The leader distributes copies of the New Game Review Sheet and guides the participants in a review of their New Game experience.

NEW GAME REVIEW SHEET

1. How did the team demonstrate desire to succeed?

2. What kinds of behavior impeded or facilitated success?

3. Who provided leadership and who exerted the most effort to achieve a satisfactory result?

4. Were challenging targets or goals established in the game?

5. What was the effect of positive feedback?

6. What was the effect of negative feedback?

7. How can the lessons from this project be applied in our normal work?

24 Organizational Role

Purpose

To assist a team in defining its role in an organization and the ways in which it relates to other significant groups. This activity is particularly relevant to teams that act in a support or service capacity.

Time

A minimum of one and one-half hours.

Materials

I. A large newsprint pad, felt-tipped markers, and masking tape, or a chalkboard and chalk.

II. Blank paper and a pencil for each participant.

Preparation

If the team is not familiar with the process used in this activity, it may want to use a consultant outside the organization who has had some experience in helping groups solve problems. The consultant's function is to help the group clarify its responses and conclusions by presenting information and by asking probing or clarifying questions.

Method

I. The leader distributes paper and pencils and asks the members to write individual responses to the following statements:
1. The contribution of this team to the health and future of the organization is:
2. In making this contribution, three (or four) activities that are unique to this group and essentially are not shared with others in the organization are:
3. Three (or four) activities that we should share with others in the organization are:

II. When each person has completed his responses, the leader or the consultant charts each contribution under the 1, 2, 3, 4 headings and posts the three lists. Then the team is allowed sufficient time to absorb the information thoroughly.

III. The team, guided by the leader, discusses the members' responses to determine:
   1. Their common characteristics;
   2. Their differences.

IV. Where differences of opinion exist, these are openly discussed with the aim of achieving consensus on one list of responses under each heading.

V. The final consensual output is the "role charter" for the team; it can be communicated to other groups in the organization.

25 Mapping the Organization

Purpose

   I.   To define a team's position within its organization and the other parts of the organization to which it relates.

   II.   To define the nature of those relationships.

Time

Up to two hours.

Materials

A large newsprint pad, felt-tipped markers in at least three colors, and masking tape, or a chalkboard and chalk.

Physical Arrangement

A room with sufficient wall space to post the team's relationship map.

Method

   I.   If there is no external consultant, the leader or a team member should serve as recorder.

   II.   The recorder explains that a map will be drawn to represent the team and its relationships with other groups. The recorder draws a circle in the center of the newsprint, explaining that it represents the team.

   III.   The team identifies other work units within the organization with which it has relationships. These are represented by drawing other, smaller circles on the newsprint, as shown in the accompanying diagram.

   IV.   The team discusses its relationships with these other groups and the recorder diagrams each of them on the chart in terms of the following:

      1. The intensity and frequency of the relationship, which can be symbolized by lines connecting the team's circle with the other circle, i.e., three lines if the relationship is frequent or important, a dotted line if it is infrequent or unimportant.

     2. The nature of the relationship, e.g., service to, input to, output from, which can be symbolized by directional arrows at the end of the relationship lines.

     3. If necessary, each relationship line can be numbered, and comments on the nature of the relationships, their purpose, and their appropriateness can be listed on a separate sheet.

V. When the map is completed, each member should check it to ensure that there is consensus and that no "related" groups are omitted.

VI. The team members then can consider the following questions and their answers are charted:

     1. Are there any other parts of the organization with which we need:
- More interaction?
- Improved interaction?
- To commence or cease interaction?

Are any members of the team particularly involved?

     2. What specifically would we like to do in order to:
- Provide a better service?
- Receive a better service?
- Make the interactions more useful or positive?

Is action a matter for the team leader, the whole team, or particular members?

Follow-Up Activities

I. The map can be shared with other teams as a means of communicating specific views about mutual interactions.

II. The map can be used as the basis for a priority list of actions the team can take to improve its relationships with other parts of the organization.

MAPPING THE ORGANIZATION

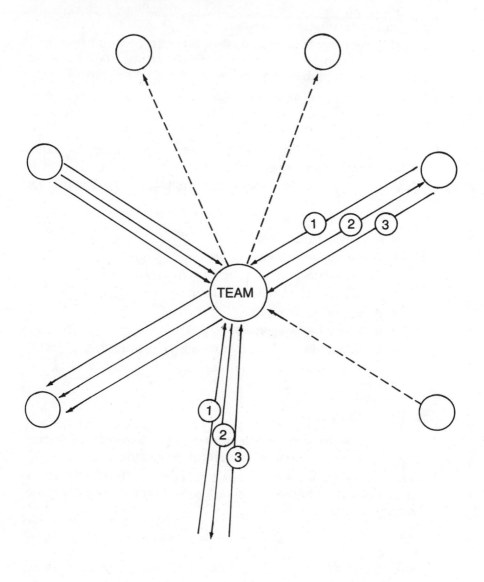

26 Team Survival

Purpose

To clarify the essential reasons for the existence of a specific team as a part of the wider organization.

Time

Two hours.

Materials

I. A large newsprint pad and felt-tipped markers, or a chalkboard and chalk.

II. Blank paper and a pencil for each participant.

Method

I. The leader presents the following briefing to the team:

A new president has just joined your organization (XYZ). He has the reputation of being a cold, hard operator. His specialization has been the cutting of costs and staff, which has achieved dramatic results in some of his past companies. However, in some cases, his company "surgery" improved performance in the short term, but caused the organization to fail.

It appears that the new president is a man of considerable energy and drive, single-minded in his purpose of cutting costs and reducing an organization to the bare minimum. It is said that the only way to influence him is with strong, well-considered, and logical argument.

In the six months he has been with XYZ, the new president has shut down whole departments with little discussion or dialogue. Rumors have been spreading that *your* team is the next one on the list. It is now 9:30 in the morning and your boss has been summoned to an 11 A.M. meeting with the president, who wants a justification of your team's existence in the organization.

II. The leader distributes paper and pencils and assigns the following tasks to the team:

1. You have one hour to prepare a presentation for the president, giving the strongest possible case for why your team is essential to the organization. Assume that if your case is not strong

enough, the whole team will be discharged from the organization.

2. In preparing the presentation, you should consider the following:
   - The goals of the wider organization.
   - Your contribution to the wider organization.
   - The cost/benefit equation in keeping or dismissing your team.
   - The consequences to the wider organization of the disbanding of your team.
   - What would happen if your team's manpower budget were slashed.

III. The maximum value will be gained if the team's presentation is as real as possible. This can be best achieved by making the presentation to a strong, forceful personality from outside the team. This individual can be briefed about the objectives of the activity and, in particular, should consider the following questions: "If I were the president who is hearing the presentation:

1. Would I want additional data?

2. Am I convinced that the team is essential to the organization as a whole? If not, what would it take to convince me?

3. What are the unique and essential contributions that the team makes?

4. Would I wish the team to improve its performance or contributions? If so, specifically in what areas?"

IV. When the presentation has been completed, the leader asks the team members to consider the following:

1. How clear you are about your team's role and contribution to the wider organization.

2. Any points of disagreement that arose in preparing the presentation.

3. What you have learned about your function.

4. Whether it would be useful to test your findings on other teams.

5. What actions you can take to improve your contribution.

How Good Are Your Meetings?

Purpose

    I.   To diagnose the problems a team has with the planning and control of its meetings.

    II.   To plan and take specific actions to overcome these problems.

Time

    A minimum of one hour.

Materials

    I.   A copy of the Meetings Questionnaire and a pencil for each participant.

    II.   A large newsprint pad and felt-tipped markers, or a chalkboard and chalk.

Method

    I.   The leader distributes the Meetings Questionnaire and pencils to the team members, asking them to read the instructions and respond to each item.

    II.   After the questionnaire is completed, the team decides whether to report the scores anonymously or orally.

   III.   The leader charts the rank order of the headings, placing those having the highest scores at the top.

   IV.   The team selects the statement with the highest single score and agrees on specific actions that can be taken to overcome the problem at the next meeting. This process is continued at successive meetings so that each problem can be worked through in descending order.

MEETINGS QUESTIONNAIRE

Instructions: Read the three scored headings and use them to evaluate each statement. Choose one score (4, 2, or 0) that corresponds to your opinion of how the statement applies to your meetings. Write the score in the appropriate blank.

	SCORE:	4 True (Usually)	2 Some- times	0 Not True (Seldom)
1. The purposes of our meetings are not defined.		_____	_____	_____
2. We do not decide what we want to achieve by the end of a meeting.		_____	_____	_____
3. People do not prepare sufficiently for our meetings.		_____	_____	_____
4. We seldom review our progress during meetings.		_____	_____	_____
5. We do not allocate meeting time well.		_____	_____	_____
6. Ideas and views often are lost or forgotten.		_____	_____	_____
7. We do not decide which agenda items have priority.		_____	_____	_____
8. We allocate equal amounts of time to trivia and important issues.		_____	_____	_____
9. We often are diverted from the matter at hand.		_____	_____	_____
10. People lose concentration and attention.		_____	_____	_____
11. Sometimes there are several meetings when there should be one.		_____	_____	_____
12. We do not review and confirm what has been agreed upon and how those decisions will be activated.		_____	_____	_____

Why / How Charting

Purpose

To help a team clarify its objectives and plan appropriate problem-solving actions.

Time

One and one-half hours.

Materials

A large newsprint pad, felt-tipped markers, and masking tape, or a chalkboard and chalk.

Method

I. The leader asks the team members to familiarize themselves with the technique of Why/How Charting by reviewing the accompanying diagram. This example is developed in outline only to illustrate the method.

II. The leader asks the group to choose a problem or task that it is facing, and he writes this in the task/problem box in the center of the newsprint pad.

III. The team members discover the reasons (goals) for pursuing the task/problem by answering the question "Why?". The leader records their answers on the upper part of the chart and continues asking why until the broad aims or purposes of the task/problem are identified and then boxed for emphasis, as shown in the diagram. As additional sheets are filled, they are posted where all can see them.

IV. The team discusses the "Goals" items to determine whether they all are necessary and to prioritize those deserving the most attention; these are boxed on the chart to indicate emphasis.

V. The team brainstorms answers to the question "How?". The leader records the suggested "Action Steps" on the lower part of the chart, writing them in the order of their priority for facilitating a plan of action. (The numbers shown in the diagram are an example of an action plan defined in priority order.)

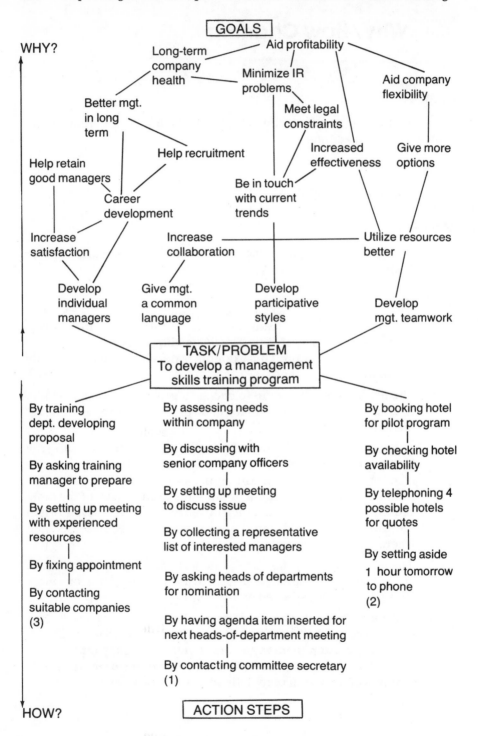

VI. After the action steps are charted, the team evaluates them by asking the following questions:
   1. Are all these actions necessary to achieve the stated goals?
   2. Are these items, taken together, sufficient?

Variations

As a further step, the team can identify other options for action by brainstorming the ideas shown in the top tier of goals.

29 Effective Problem-Solving Survey

Purpose

I. To identify strengths and weaknesses in team problem solving.

II. To set agendas for strengthening the weakest characteristics.

Time

Forty-five minutes.

Materials

I. One copy of the Effective Problem-Solving Survey for each participant.

II. A large newsprint pad and felt-tipped markers, or a chalkboard and chalk.

III. Blank paper and a pencil for each participant.

Method

I. The leader distributes one copy of the Effective Problem-Solving Survey, paper, and a pencil to each member. He tells the members to read the instructions and complete the survey. (Five minutes.)

II. After the survey has been completed, the leader asks whether the participants want to report their individual scores orally or write them down and turn them in anonymously.

III. The leader collects the scores, charts them, and identifies the two items with the lowest scores. (Ten minutes.)

IV. The members discuss the problem items and identify six action steps that could help the group improve in these two areas. The leader charts the suggestions; he makes them available for reference at the next working session. (Thirty minutes.)

EFFECTIVE PROBLEM-SOLVING SURVEY

Instructions. Please give your candid opinion of your team's most recent problem-solving session by rating its characteristics on the seven-point scales shown below. Circle the appropriate number on each scale to represent your evaluation.

Lacked order and poorly controlled	1	2	3	4	5	6	7	Orderly and well controlled
Confusion about objectives	1	2	3	4	5	6	7	Clear and shared objectives
Organization inappropriate to task	1	2	3	4	5	6	7	Organization was flexible, appropriate to task
Criteria for success not established	1	2	3	4	5	6	7	Clear criteria for success established
Information was poorly evaluated	1	2	3	4	5	6	7	Information was well analyzed
Planning was inadequate	1	2	3	4	5	6	7	Planning was effective, thorough
Action was ineffective	1	2	3	4	5	6	7	Action was effective, adequate
No attempt to learn from the experience	1	2	3	4	5	6	7	Thorough review to help team learn from experience
Time was wasted	1	2	3	4	5	6	7	Time was well used
People withdrew or became negative	1	2	3	4	5	6	7	Everyone participated positively

30 Team Mission and Individual Objectives

Purpose

I.   To help clarify the team's mission to team members.

II. To test for strengths or problems in the ways that team members relate their individual goals to the team's overall mission.

Time

Half an hour for individual preparation. One hour for team discussion. It may require two or more discussion sessions to achieve a satisfactory outcome.

Materials

I.   A copy each of the Team's Mission Sheet and the Individual Objectives Sheet, and a pencil for each participant.

II. A large newsprint pad, felt-tipped markers, and masking tape, or a chalkboard and chalk.

Method

I.   The team meets briefly to begin the preparatory work for the main team meeting. The leader distributes copies of the Team's Mission Sheet and the Individual Objectives Sheet to each of the members and asks the members to complete the sheets and bring them to the next meeting.

II. At the second meeting, each team member is asked to read his statement of the team's mission.

III. The individual Team's Mission Sheets are displayed, then the team members review all contributions and work to compile a statement of the team's mission(s) with which the whole team agrees.

IV. Each team member outlines for the team his individual objectives and, in the light of the statement of the team's mission(s), reviews the appropriateness of these objectives.

V. If it is clear that some objectives are no longer appropriate in relation to the team's mission(s), the meeting is adjourned to allow the members to review their objectives. The team schedules a meeting within one month of the original meeting, at which time it will consider objectives again.

TEAM'S MISSION SHEET

The major reasons for the existence of this team are to achieve the following:

INDIVIDUAL OBJECTIVES SHEET

Over the next (six months, nine months, one year, two years, as appropriate) I wish to achieve the following in my work:

Statement of desired achievement	By what date	How I will know I have succeeded	Part of team's mission it relates to
1.			
2.			

31 Team Communications

Purpose

   I.   To identify specific malfunctions in team communication.

  II.   To plan actions to correct the team-communication malfunctions.

Time

One and one-half hours, plus individual preparation.

Materials

   I.   A large newsprint pad, felt-tipped markers, and masking tape, or a chalkboard and chalk.

  II.   Blank paper and a pencil for each participant.

Method

   I.   The leader distributes paper and a pencil to each participant and charts the following information on newsprint for the participants to read:

TEAM COMMUNICATIONS

Three examples of communication malfunction in the team

Example	Effect it had on me
1.	
2.	
3.	

II.   The leader instructs the participants to follow the outline shown in the Team Communications chart and write statements defining three specific examples of communication difficulties.

III. The participants report their team communication statements to the leader and he writes them on the newsprint chart.

IV. The leader helps the team to consider each of these statements and to:

1. Identify any communication malfunctions that are similar in cause or effect.

2. List them in order of priority.

3. Discuss and decide specifically what should be done to prevent their occurrence in the future.

 **Start Up**

Purpose

I. To examine different work roles and methods of organization.

II. To observe how each member's contribution fits into the team's overall effort.

Time

A minimum of one and one-half hours, including the review.

Materials

I. Copies of the Start Up Briefing Sheet and the Start Up Review Sheet and a pencil for each participant.

II. A large newsprint pad and felt-tipped markers, or a chalkboard and chalk.

Method

I. A copy of the Start Up Briefing Sheet and a pencil are distributed to each of the participants. (Use of the briefing sheets can be eliminated by displaying the briefing information on the newsprint pad or chalkboard.)

II. After the participants read the briefing sheet, the leader or a team member directs them to start the assignment.

III. When the time is up, the leader distributes the Start Up Review Sheets and instructs the participants to complete them.

IV. The participants discuss their experience, using their review sheets. (Forty minutes.)

START UP BRIEFING SHEET

Your team has just been given a new assignment which could be the break you are all looking for. Your firm has purchased a new factory to produce a dog food using the impressive new "Freshchunk" process. The firm is sure that it can make a good dent in the pet food market. The factory is equipped but not staffed; it needs 120 operators to operate. Your team has been assigned to set up and run the operation for a year. You have fifty minutes to discuss the problem and answer the following questions:

1. What work role and what job title should each team member have?

2. How will the management group plan and make the numerous decisions needed in setting up the operation?

3. How will you clarify roles and resolve disputes?

4. What will be the pattern of your meetings in the first two months?

START UP REVIEW SHEET

1. Are you satisfied with your roles?

2. Do you feel that the chosen management style will be effective?

3. Is the communication pattern sufficient?

4. Do you feel satisfied with the suggestions about the clarification of roles and the resolution of disputes?

5. Do you feel confident that the team can handle the new factory?

33 How Do We Make Decisions?

Purpose

I.   To examine how the team and individual members typically make decisions.

II. To plan changes in the team's decision-making process.

Time

One hour or more.

Materials

I.   A copy each of the Decision-Making Check List and the Decision-Making Interpretation Chart, and a pencil for each participant.

II. A large newsprint pad and felt-tipped markers, or chalkboard and chalk.

Background

One of the most important questions regarding decision making is "Who actually decides?" From answers to this question, five different types of decision making can be clearly identified.

1. *Individual Decision.* One person, normally the boss, actually makes a decision, and others who are involved in the situation are expected to abide by the decision.

2. *Minority Decisions.* A few of those involved in a situation meet to consider the matter and make a decision, and this is binding for all concerned.

3. *Majority Decisions.* More than half of those involved in a situation make a decision and this is binding for all concerned. Many political and democratic organizations use this principle.

4. *Consensus Decisions.* An entire group considers a problem on a basis of reason and discussion. Each member expresses a view and a decision is made to which all can commit themselves at least in part.

5. *Unanimous Decisions.* Each person fully agrees on the action to be taken, and everyone concerned can fully subscribe to the decision taken.

When people are involved in making a decision, they are much more likely to be committed to that decision than if some other person, or small group, makes a decision on their behalf. Therefore, going up the aforementioned decision-making scale (from Individual Decisions to Unanimous Decisions) increases commitment, although it also increases the difficulty of coming to an agreement.

Method

I. The leader introduces the activity using the background information provided here.

II. The leader gives each participant a copy each of the Decision-Making Check List and the Decision-Making Interpretation Chart and a pencil.

III. The participants complete the Decision-Making Check List and the Decision-Making Interpretation Chart.

IV. The leader instructs the individual participants each to choose the style of decision-making he prefers for team meetings, and then share this choice with the group, giving brief reasons for his preference.

V. While the preferences are presented, the leader charts them on the newsprint pad, showing their frequency and rank order.

VI. The leader directs the participants to choose a decision-making style for their team, and he guides them through the following steps:

1. If there are differences in the individual preferences, the team works to resolve them and to reach a decision on an appropriate style.
   - When the decision has been made, the team identifies the style by which it was reached.
   - Then the team works to identify three or more actions which could be taken in the next meeting to ensure that the chosen style will succeed.

2. If there is unanimity in the individual preferences, the team identifies three or more actions which can be taken in the next meeting to ensure that the preferred style will work.

DECISION-MAKING CHECK LIST

Instructions: Think about your typical ways of making decisions, then read each of the statements below and choose five that are most typical for you. Mark these, and when you have completed your selection, look at the Decision-Making Interpretation Chart.

1. When decision making is necessary, a few of us usually get together and take care of it.

2. The senior person usually decides and that is it.

3. People really get a chance to express their views.

4. Typically, everyone agrees somewhat with decisions taken.

5. We frequently decide on the basis of majority opinion.

6. One person is in charge and effectually makes decisions.

7. Often everyone freely agrees with decisions and supports them wholeheartedly.

8. There is a small clique that runs things around here.

9. Decisions are made when most people decide on a particular course of action.

10. We would not make a decision until everyone is completely in agreement.

11. People are free to air their views but the boss decides.

12. A few people usually dominate the group.

13. Decisions are not made unless everyone can accept proposals to some extent.

14. A numerical majority is required before decisions are made.

15. Each member actively supports decisions.

DECISION-MAKING INTERPRETATION CHART

After you have marked five statements, circle the statement numbers in the first column shown below, then total each row. The highest scores represent the typical decision-making styles of your group.

STATEMENT NUMBERS	TOTALS	STYLE
2 - 6 - 11		Individual Dominance
1 - 8 - 12		Minority Influence
5 - 9 - 14		Majority Democracy
3 - 4 - 13		Consensus
7 - 10 - 15		Unanimous View

34 Like and Don't Like

Purpose

I. To help a team initiate a critical appraisal of its functioning.

II. To allow team members to define their basic likes and dislikes about the team.

III. To plan actions for strengthening the positive and changing the negative team characteristics.

Time

One hour.

Materials

I. A copy of the Like and Don't Like Sheet and a pencil for each participant.

II. A large newsprint pad, felt-tipped markers, and masking tape, or a chalkboard and chalk.

Method

I. The leader distributes the Like and Don't Like Sheets and pencils to the team members. The members are directed to write up to six responses to complete each of the two statements shown on the sheet.

II. After the sheets are completed, the leader asks the participants whether they want to share their responses orally with the group and clarify or explain their reasons for making each statement or would prefer to submit the sheets anonymously for a more general discussion.

III. If the sheets are submitted, they are displayed. Common factors are identified by the team. The leader charts the most frequently expressed "likes" and "don't likes."

IV. The team suggests actions that can be taken to strengthen the positive and change the negative factors. The leader helps the team to determine a priority list of actions to be taken.

LIKE AND DON'T LIKE SHEET

What I like about this team is:

1.

2.

3.

4.

5.

6.

What I don't like about this team is:

1.

2.

3.

4.

5.

6.

35 The Best and the Worst

Purpose

I. To look back and identify the best and the worst aspects of the team's performance over a specific period.

II. To identify and share ideas on why these aspects existed.

III. To develop team consensus on future actions to reinforce the positive and overcome the negative features of the team's operation.

Time

One and one-half hours.

Materials

I. A copy of The Best and the Worst Activity Sheet and a pencil for each participant.

II. A large newsprint pad and felt-tipped markers, or a chalkboard and chalk.

Method

I. The leader distributes The Best and the Worst Activity Sheet and a pencil to each participant. He directs the members to complete the lists under each heading.

II. The team decides whether to sign the sheets or submit them anonymously.

III. The leader charts each sheet, and the team identifies the items of agreement and explores the areas of difference. The team attempts to reach consensus on at least three negative and three positive features of the team's operation.

IV. The team determines one action it will take in the next month in order to overcome the *negative* factors and one action it will take to reinforce or improve the *positive* features.

THE BEST AND THE WORST ACTIVITY SHEET

Name_____ Period Under Review_____

During the period under review, the five best things this team has achieved are:

1.

2.

3.

4.

5.

During the same period, the five worst failures or mistakes of the team have been:

1.

2.

3.

4.

5.

㉖ You Should Have Been a . . .

Purpose

To facilitate the sharing of constructive feedback between team members.

Time

Approximately one hour.

Materials

I. One copy of the You Should Have Been a . . . Activity Sheet and a pencil for each participant.

II. A large newsprint pad, felt-tipped markers, and masking tape, or a chalkboard and chalk.

III. Blank paper for each participant.

Method

I. The leader distributes a copy of the You Should Have Been a . . . Activity Sheet and a pencil to each of the members, asking them to read the instructions and complete the statements.

II. After the sheets are completed, the leader asks the team members to read out their descriptions. The leader summarizes the description for each member on a newsprint sheet with the member's name on it, identifying who has given each description. This results in a series of "should have been" descriptions for each team member on a separate sheet.

III. The feedback sheets for each member are posted, and five minutes is given for each member to review the descriptions given for him.

IV. The review period is followed by an open session, in which each team member can ask questions of the authors of his "should have been" descriptions. The aim should be to allow the other persons to clarify their feelings and reasons for making the descriptions.

V. A variation or extension of this can be for each team member to select a "should have been" description that he finds particularly interesting and to spend ten to fifteen minutes with the person who made the description, while that member explains his reasons for making the description.

VI. At the end of the discussion period, the leader distributes blank paper and tells each member to complete a list headed "What I have learned about others' perceptions of me." These lists are shared with the whole team and discussed, or may be retained privately by the individual, if he does not wish to share.

Note

This activity is best conducted by an experienced team leader or facilitator. The purpose of this activity is to provide *helpful* and *constructive* feedback. Therefore, the members should be careful in giving feedback and offer their evaluations of individuals in constructive, specific, and action-related items. Before they start, it probably will help the team members to review Activity 1, "Giving Feedback."

YOU SHOULD HAVE BEEN A . . . ACTIVITY SHEET

Think about other individuals in the team and complete the following statement for each of them.

If _____were starting his career again

and chose to enter a profession other than his present one, he should

have been a_____because

37 Is It OK To Be More Me?

Introduction

Personal strength is often reduced by role playing and unauthentic behavior. A manager seeking to decrease the differences between his personal behavior and genuine feelings will try to behave naturally and not be inhibited by fears and needs for approval.

Successful (and likeable) managers may differ greatly in their approaches but they usually share a genuine respect for their own visions. They are prepared to be themselves and to take responsibility for their actions. They know their own capacity and work vigorously within what they perceive as their limits.

Well-developed managers realize their own unique personalities and work through personal problems until clear resolutions are achieved. As a result, they emerge with authentic, spontaneous, and personal styles. They are themselves.

Purpose

To assist an individual in identifying:

- What kinds of past influences affect his behavior; and
- Whether he wants to change any aspects of his current behavior patterns.

Time

Approximately one hour.

Materials

Blank paper and a pencil for each participant.

Method

I. This activity should be completed by an individual, working alone, in a quiet place free from interruptions. On the left hand

---

Adapted from "Is It OK to be More Me?" in Mike Woodcock and Dave Francis, *"Unblocking Your Organization."* La Jolla, CA: University Associates, 1979, p. 222. Used with permission of the publishers.

side of the paper, the person should list the principal "shoulds" that affect his behavior, such as:

- I should be successful.
- I should be nice.
- I should not argue with the boss.

II. When the list is completed, the participant should look at each item and identify, as far as possible, where these injunctions came from (for example, from parents, teachers, a boss, peers, an organization, a culture, a church, etc.).

III. Next to each item on the list, the participant writes what his inclination would be if the injunction had not been present and whether this new statement "feels right."

IV. The participant should find an individual who knows him well and explain the meaning of the items on the list. The second person is invited to comment. While he is speaking, the participant who made the list should try to confine any interruptions to questions of clarification. In particular, he should try to avoid being defensive and notice when a defensive attitude arises.

Managing People Skills Inventory

Purpose

I. To provide a systematic basis for a manager's self-evaluation and for team feedback on individual managerial skills.

II. To identify priorities for individual development of managerial skills.

Time

A minimum of one hour.

Materials

One copy of the Managing People Skills Inventory and a pencil for each participant.

Background

Prior to undertaking this session it is helpful to the team if it has completed Activity 39, "Good Coaching Practice."

Method

I. After distributing a copy of the Managing People Skills Inventory and a pencil to each team member, the leader instructs the members to complete the inventory within twenty minutes.

II. After twenty minutes, the leader directs the participants to share their scores with at least one other team member and ask for feedback. He suggests that mutual counseling can be useful to the participants. (A minimum of forty minutes.)

Adapted from A. G. Banet, Consultation-Skills Inventory. In J. W. Pfeiffer and J. E. Jones (Eds.). *The 1976 Annual Handbook for Group Facilitators.* La Jolla, CA: University Associates, 1976.

MANAGING PEOPLE SKILLS INVENTORY

Instructions: This check list is designed to help you think about important behaviors undertaken by management. It gives you an opportunity to assess your own behavior and skills. To use the inventory best:

1. Read through the list of behaviors and decide which ones you are doing the right amount of, which ones you need to do more, and which ones you need to do less of. Mark a check [√] for each item in the appropriate place.

2. Some behaviors that are important to you may not be listed here. Write the unlisted behaviors in the blank spaces provided.

3. Ignore items that are irrelevant to your job.

4. Go back and review the list and select three or four behaviors in which you want most to improve. List these in the following spaces and then discuss these with at least one other participant.

My personal priorities are:

1. _____

2. _____

3. _____

4. _____

	OK	Need More	Need Less
Relationships Upwards			
1. Competing with my peers	____	____	____
2. Being open with my seniors	____	____	____
3. Feeling inferior to colleagues	____	____	____
4. Standing up for myself	____	____	____
5. Building open relationships	____	____	____
6. Following policy guidelines	____	____	____
7. Questioning policy guidelines	____	____	____
_____	____	____	____
_____	____	____	____
_____	____	____	____

My Team	OK	Need More	Need Less
8. Knowing other team members as individuals	___	___	___
9. Meeting sufficiently often	___	___	___
10. Supporting open expression of views	___	___	___
11. Setting high standards	___	___	___
12. Punishing behavior that deviates from the team norm	___	___	___
13. Clarifying aims/objectives	___	___	___
14. Giving information and my views	___	___	___
15. Using status to influence decisions with the team	___	___	___
16. Delegating to reduce workload	___	___	___
_____	___	___	___
_____	___	___	___
_____	___	___	___
_____	___	___	___

One-to-One

	OK	Need More	Need Less
17. Helping others identify problems	___	___	___
18. Practicing counseling skills	___	___	___
19. Being distant with some people	___	___	___
20. Intervening when things go wrong	___	___	___
21. Being strong when reprimanding	___	___	___
22. Giving energy to others	___	___	___
23. Clarifying individual objectives	___	___	___
24. Supporting others in difficulties	___	___	___
25. Bringing problems out	___	___	___
26. Supporting risk taking	___	___	___
27. Being open on assessment of others	___	___	___
_____	___	___	___
_____	___	___	___
_____	___	___	___
_____	___	___	___

Relationships with the Work Force

	OK	Need More	Need Less
28. Being known as a person by employees	___	___	___
29. Being available to employees	___	___	___

	OK	Need More	Need Less
30. Knowing how people feel	___	___	___
31. Acting to resolve conflicts	___	___	___
32. Emphasizing communication	___	___	___
33. Passing information quickly	___	___	___
34. Emphasizing personal status	___	___	___
35. Bypassing management structure when communicating	___	___	___
_____	___	___	___
_____	___	___	___
_____	___	___	___
_____	___	___	___

Working in Groups

	OK	Need More	Need Less
36. Using a systematic approach	___	___	___
37. Developing others' skills	___	___	___
38. Being prompt	___	___	___
39. Using time effectively	___	___	___
40. Listening actively	___	___	___
41. Openly expressing my views	___	___	___
42. Dominating others	___	___	___
43. Maintaining good group climate.	___	___	___
44. Dealing constructively with disruptive behavior	___	___	___
45. Building informal contacts	___	___	___
46. Disparaging other groups	___	___	___
47. Sharing objectives with other groups	___	___	___
48. Identifying mutual communication needs	___	___	___
49. Arranging intergroup social events	___	___	___
50. Acting to resolve conflicts	___	___	___
_____	___	___	___
_____	___	___	___
_____	___	___	___
_____	___	___	___

	OK	Need More	Need Less

Training and Development

51. Making time for counseling
52. Identifying the group's training needs
53. Setting coaching assignments
54. Allocating time and money for training
55. Giving feedback to others
56. Sharing parts of my job for others' development

Continuous Self-Development

57. Setting aside time to think
58. Visiting other organizations
59. Discussing principles and values
60. Taking on new challenges
61. Attending training events
62. Knowing when and how to use specialist resources

39 Good Coaching Practice

Purpose

I. To identify the skills of good coaching practice.

II. To allow a group to set standards for its own performance.

Time

Approximately one hour.

Materials

I. One copy of the Good Coaching Practice Check List and a pencil for each participant.

II. A large newsprint pad, felt-tipped markers, and masking tape, or chalkboard and chalk.

Physical Arrangement

A room large enough to accommodate a circle of chairs for each group with the groups sufficiently separated to allow privacy.

Method

I. The leader explains that the purpose of the activity is to help the group identify the characteristics of good coaching. Coaching is defined as *intentionally helping another person to improve his competence by using development opportunities at work.* The leader writes this definition on a sheet of newsprint and displays it as a reminder during the session.

II. The leader randomly divides the participants into two or three subgroups and asks that each group seat its members in a circle and separate the circles to allow some privacy.

III. A copy of the Good Coaching Practice Check List and a pencil are distributed to each participant.

IV. The leader instructs the subgroups to read the check list instructions and complete the assignment in thirty minutes.

V. When the time is up, the subgroups meet together and share their lists. The leader displays a large list on the newsprint pad, indicating by tally the items deleted, and writing in the items added by the subgroups.

VI. Using a consensus method of decision making the leader helps the team to compile one check list. (Approximately twenty minutes.)

VII. The leader has the final list typed and distributes it to all team members under the heading "Our Guidelines for Coaching."

VIII. Since the team has identified a framework for assessing coaching sessions, further understanding and skills can only be acquired by practice. One way to develop the members' skills is to invite into coaching sessions, with voluntary agreement of all involved, an observer who uses the team's check list and gives feedback after the session.

GOOD COACHING PRACTICE CHECK LIST

Instructions: Listed below are some coaching characteristics generally considered to be significant. However, you may not agree that all the items are appropriate. Consider each statement and if you decide to delete it, draw a line through it. Since the list is incomplete, you may want to add statements of coaching characteristics that you find helpful. Write these items in the space provided at the end of the list.

1. The coach adopts a friendly attitude toward the coaching participant.
2. The coaching discussion is confidential.
3. Steps are taken by the coach to prevent interruptions of the coaching session.
4. The discussion begins by checking out what both people are seeking to achieve.
5. The coach spends a good proportion of the available discussion time in active listening.
6. The coach frequently summarizes and checks back.
7. Relevant information is fully discussed.
8. Feelings can be openly expressed.
9. Problems are jointly analyzed and assessed.
10. Options are identified and their benefits explicitly evaluated.
11. There is a strong emphasis on action and plans are made.
12. Opportunities for personal development are intentionally sought.
13. A date is established to follow up on the session.
14. The meeting is reviewed so that both people can learn from the experience.
15.
16.
17.
18.
19.
20.

④⓪ Team Brainstorming

Purpose

    I.   To practice a means of generating ideas.

   II.   To develop skills in creative problem solving.

Time

One hour.

Materials

A large newsprint pad, felt-tipped markers, and masking tape, or a chalkboard and chalk.

Method

    I.   The leader states a problem to be considered by the team (see Suggested Brainstorming Problems), defining it in terms of "How to . . . ," and presents the following rules for brainstorming:

    1. There will be no criticism during the brainstorming.

    2. All ideas, no matter how ridiculous, are encouraged.

    3. As many ideas as possible should be produced.

   II.   The leader lists all the ideas generated.

  III.   At the end of the brainstorming, the leader tells the team to evaluate the ideas produced, using the following processes:

    1. Clustering ideas that are similar.

    2. Evaluating the ideas produced in terms of:

       • Value/benefit

       • Cost

       • Feasibility

       • Resources needed

  IV.   The leader posts the final listing of evaluated ideas, and the team determines their order of priority.

SUGGESTED BRAINSTORMING PROBLEMS

1. No team is perfect; they all can be improved. The task to brainstorm is: "How to make this team better."

2. There are members who seldom speak at group meetings. The task to brainstorm is: "How to encourage and allow more reticent members to participate in group meetings."

3. The volunteers who give their own time to a community group do not want to waste that time. The task to brainstorm is: "How to plan meeting agendas for the most economical and efficient use of the group members' time?"

4. The mugging of people in large cities is an increasingly universal problem. The task to brainstorm is: "How to reduce muggings."

5. Etc.

41 Creative Change

Purpose

I. To study the stages in a creative process.

II. To use the creative process to accomplish real benefits for the team.

Materials

I. A large newsprint pad and felt-tipped markers, or a chalkboard and chalk.

II. Blank paper and a pencil for each participant.

Method

I. The leader presents a briefing on the creativity project, outlining the steps to be taken and making the following points:

- The team is going to participate in a project entitled, Identify and Materially Improve Our Working Environment.

- The project will last six weeks.

- The project will be considered successful only when measurable improvements have been made.

II. The leader distributes paper and pencils to the team members and leads them through the following activities:

Step One: Visioning. Each individual spends ten minutes privately noting down his answers to the question, "What is your ideal environment for work, assuming that there are no practical limitations?" (Ten minutes.)

Step Two: Assembling. Each individual list is read aloud and the leader lists the ideas, no matter how bizarre, on the newsprint pad. (Twenty-five minutes.)

Step Three: Selecting. Each individual is given three votes to be used for the following question: "Which of the ideas suggested would you most like to see implemented in practice?" The votes are recorded next to each item chosen, then these items are listed in rank order with the item receiving the most votes placed at the top. (Fifteen minutes.)

Step Four: Planning. The team uses the criterion "Which of these ideas can be put into practice by six weeks from today?" to select, by consensus, the three most practical ideas.

The next task for the team is turning these ideas into objectives, i.e., time-bound and measurable statements of intended achievement.

The team can analyze the benefits and possible problems of an idea by using a chart like the one shown here. The group should take ten minutes to analyze each idea and list as many helping and hindering forces as possible. (Forty-five minutes.)

Helping Forces	Hindering Forces
1. _____	1. _____
2. _____	2. _____
3. _____	3. _____
4. _____	4. _____

Step Five: Action. The members select one idea that looks most useful for their team and list ways of adding to the helping forces and reducing the influence of the hindering forces. They can use Activity 40, "Team Brainstorming" or Activity 28, "Why/How Charting" to set individual and team goals for action. The team agrees to review its progress in approximately six weeks. (Twenty-five minutes or more.)

42 Creative Presentation

Purpose

I.   To help group members identify the creative strength of their team and themselves.

II. To study how team members work together on a problem-solving task.

Time

Approximately two hours, including time for review.

Materials

I.   It helps to use a C120 cassette tape and a tape recorder with a counter (this can be set at zero prior to the "broadcast").

II. A large newsprint pad and felt-tipped markers, or a chalkboard and chalk.

Physical Arrangement

I.   A quiet room.

II. A table near an electrical outlet.

Method

I.   The leader writes the following assignment on the newsprint pad and announces it to the team: "Your income depends on your ability to market yourself as a group that can help organizations solve their problems. Prepare a five-minute script advertising the strengths of your team and then record this presentation on tape. You have fifty-five minutes to complete the entire task, but you may not begin recording for forty-five minutes, that is, until ten minutes before the end of the assigned time."

II. As soon as the project is announced, the tape recorder is started. The tape records the development of the project, and then is used for the five-minute advertising program.

III. When the program has been completed, the team invites people from outside the team to listen to the broadcast and comment on the presentation.

IV. Following the guests' comments, the tape is rewound to the beginning, and the team members listen to their development process. They attempt to identify the strengths of each group member, and the leader lists these separately on the newsprint pad. (One hour.)

43 Organizational Mirror

Purpose

I. To bring two teams together for mutual and self-analysis.

II. To help the teams share these perceptions.

III. To suggest changes or developments that would be beneficial to joint effectiveness.

Time

Two hours.

Physical Arrangement

At least two rooms are required, one large enough for both teams, and one in which one of the groups can meet separately.

Materials

Large newsprint pads and felt-tipped markers, or chalkboards and chalk, for each group.

Method

I. It is desirable to enlist the help of an external facilitator, whose role would be to explain the activity to the groups and assist with the discussions.

II. The facilitator asks each team to consider the following questions for forty-five minutes:

1. How do we view the other group?
2. How do we think they view us?
3. How do we view ourselves?
4. What would we like them to do:
   - More of
   - Less of
   - The same

The teams are directed to separate rooms to carry out this part of the activity. Each team is asked to record its conclusions on a newsprint pad for presentation to the other team.

III. The two groups reassemble in the joint meeting room, and each team presents its views to the other group. At this stage, there should be little discussion or questioning. (Thirty minutes.)

IV. After the two presentations are made, time should be allowed for questioning in order to clarify any possible misinterpretations.

V. The facilitator helps the two groups discuss the data, with the purpose of reaching consensus on the question, "What can we do together to improve our joint effectiveness?" The emphasis should be on commitment to action. (Forty-five minutes.)

44 Circles of Influence

Purpose

To use a systematic approach to evaluate the forces influencing a team and to plan ways to increase its strength and influence.

Time

At least one hour.

Materials

A large newsprint pad, felt-tipped markers, and masking tape, or a chalkboard and chalk.

Method

I. The leader introduces the session by drawing the diagram shown here on newsprint and posting it. The team then discusses the concept to assure a shared understanding.

Circles of Influence Diagram

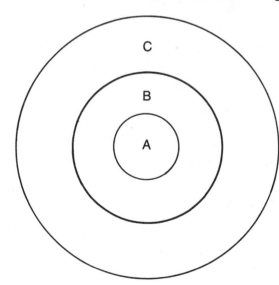

Circle A represents problems that can be solved completely by the team.

Circle B represents problems that the team can influence but cannot completely control.

Circle C represents problems or forces affecting the team that are outside its influence.

II. Each team member is asked to spend ten minutes listing the problems affecting the team at the present time.

III. When the lists are completed, they are passed to the leader, or one member, who charts the problems and asks for clarification of any vague points.

IV. Each problem is discussed to determine whether it comes within circles of influence A, B, or C. When the team reaches consensus, its decision is recorded on the diagram as a brief title or code letter.

V. The group brainstorms methods for extending the boundaries of circles A and B to increase the group's influence over the forces that impact on its performance. One member can be appointed to record these ideas on the newsprint pad.

45 Castles in the Air

Purpose

I. To experience group problem solving.

II. To explore relationships between groups.

III. To investigate management style.

Time

Three and one-half hours.

Materials

I. One Castle-Building Kit, containing the following items, for each team:

1 package of paper table napkins	1 pair of scissors
1 dozen assorted buttons	1 ball of string
1 package of paper baking cups	1 box of colored crayons
100 small index cards (3 " x 5 ")	1 roll of transparent tape
100 large index cards (5 " x 7 ")	4 table tennis balls
1 box of large paper clips	50 pipe cleaners

1 packet of assorted balloons (same number of balloons for each team).

II. A large newsprint pad, felt-tipped markers, and masking tape for each group.

Physical Arrangement

A large room with space enough for each team to meet and work privately without distraction, or one large meeting room plus a separate room for each team.

Method

I. The leader forms teams of between five and seven members. (This activity is particularly useful when the teams consist of members from different work units or departments.)

257

II. Each team is given a Castle-Building Kit and the following assignment: "Using only the materials in your kit, construct a castle at least two feet tall and make it as imaginative as possible. You have one hour to complete this assignment."

III. Each team is given space (or a separate room) in which to construct a castle. It is helpful to add an observer, or use a tape recorder, to record the problem-solving activity of the group.

IV. At the end of the one-hour period, the leader gives each team a designation by counting them off in order: A, B, C, etc. He then tells them that each team will spend the next ten minutes examining another team's castle and evaluating it for imaginative effort. Team A will evaluate Team B's castle; Team B will evaluate Team C's castle, etc., with the last team evaluating Team A's castle. The leader tells the teams that they may use their own criteria for evaluation.

V. At the end of the ten-minute evaluation period, the leader announces that each team is to select one of its members to join the team just evaluated and assist it in improving its model. Twenty minutes is allowed for this stage.

VI. In order to get maximum learning from the experience, the group now analyzes how it worked on the project. Small groups of four people are formed, each containing a balance of representatives from each project team. They are given twenty minutes to discuss the following questions:
    1. How well did your team function during the initial problem-solving task?
    2. How did you feel about the evaluation from the other group?
    3. How did the representative from the evaluation group affect your team?
    4. How do you regard the evaluation team now?

VII. Each team reassembles to analyze individual results, review either the observer's notes or a tape recording, and complete the following assignment:

"Identify and chart factors that either can help or hinder intergroup relationships. Use this information to prepare a five-minute report for presentation to the other group(s). You have fifty minutes for your review and to prepare the presentation."

VIII. Each team makes its five-minute presentation and displays its chart.

 Cartoon Time

Purpose

I. To experience the intergroup dynamics involved in the accomplishment of a creative task.

II. To assess the individual and group behavior that helped to accomplish a creative task (functional behaviors) or hindered successful accomplishment (dysfunctional behaviors).

Time

From one and one-half to two hours.

Materials

I. For each participant: one copy of the essay "Intergroup Relations" (see section 12 of Part 3).

II. For each group: one copy each of the Cartoon Time Briefing Sheet and the Cartoon Time Review Sheet, one book of drawing paper, one set of colored pens, one roll of transparent tape, blank paper, and a pencil.

III. A large newsprint pad, felt-tipped markers, and masking tape, or chalkboard and chalk.

Physical Arrangement

A room large enough to accommodate a circle of chairs for each group with the groups sufficiently separated to allow privacy.

Method

I. The leader distributes a copy of the Intergroup Relations essay to each participant and introduces the activity by covering the major points made in the essay. The participants are allowed enough time to assimilate the information.

II. The leader divides the participants into equally-sized groups of four to six members and asks each group to sit in a circle separated enough from other groups to allow privacy for each group.

III. Each group receives one copy of the Cartoon Time Briefing Sheet, one book of drawing paper, one set of colored pens, one roll of transparent tape, paper, and a pencil.

IV. The leader instructs the groups to read the briefing sheet and complete the assignment within fifty minutes.

V. After the cartoon book is submitted to the leader, a copy of the Cartoon Time Review Sheet is given to each group. The leader directs the groups to complete the review sheet in twenty-five minutes.

VI. While the groups report their reviews, the leader lists their responses on the newsprint pad.

VII. The participants share their experiences and deal with difficulties and misunderstandings that have occurred.

VIII. The cartoon book is displayed.

IX. Later, the leader sends copies of the book to the participants.

CARTOON TIME BRIEFING SHEET

In cooperation with the other group (or groups) prepare a book of cartoons illustrating the hazards of poor intergroup relationships. Work on this book should combine the efforts of all groups involved. Your group may send only one person at any time to the other group(s) for liaison purposes. You have fifty minutes to complete this task. The cartoon book will be photocopied later as a memento for each participant.

CARTOON TIME REVIEW SHEET

1. How did your group work with the other group(s)? (Did you negotiate, fight, collaborate, etc.?)

2. How much communication occurred between the involved groups?

3. What behaviors helped the groups create the cartoon book?

4. What behaviors hindered the groups in creating the cartoon book?

5. How did your group perceive the other group? How did you feel about the other group?

6. How do you think the other group perceived and felt about your group?

7. Examine the cartoon book and determine whether one group had more input than the other(s)? If it did, can you say why?

8. How would you like to work with another group if you were assigned to a similar project?